Scri

The World at Our Feet

Edited by Donna Samworth

YoungWriters in association with Lexibook

First published in Great Britain in 2004 by
YOUNG WRITERS
Remus House,
Coltsfoot Drive,
Peterborough, PE2 9JX
Telephone (01733) 890066

SB ISBN 1 84460 323 7

Foreword

Perhaps no period in life is more fertile, more vibrant with the promise of unlimited imaginative potential that the crucial formative years preceding the onset of adolescence. This volume aims to encapsulate at least some of the flavour of these exciting, sometimes tumultuous years, presenting the best of a generally excellent sample of poetry submitted by a broad cross-section of seven to eleven-year-olds for our Scribbler! The World At Our Feet Vol I *competition in 2003.*

The following poems encompass an entertaining and diverse range of themes as the children within express their hopes for the future, visualise their wildest dreams of fame and celebrity and dream of a better world, vanquished of today's evils of war and poverty. As the children of today grow into the adults of tomorrow, we hope Scribbler! The World At Our Feet Vol I *will grow to provide a valuable poetic snapshot of the thoughts, aspirations and dreams of a generation of children as they stand on the threshold of achieving their destiny.*

Donna Samworth
Editor

Contents

Untitled

Accept each other is what I think
Whether you're black or white or totally skint
It shouldn't matter if you believe in God
Or Allah or fairies you shouldn't be odd.
It's not a worry if you wear green clothes
Or have spots on your face, or a very large nose.
It isn't strange if you cannot talk
Or have no arms or cannot walk
It's not a sin to be a twin
Or if your name is Sinead Quinn
So by now you've probably got the idea
We are all humans and we all live here.

John Waters (11)

1ST PRIZE

LEXIBOOK POWER ACADEMY
AN INNOVATIVE AND PORTABLE EDUCATIONAL COMPUTER WITH HIGH RESOLUTION LCD DISPLAY, GRAPHICS AND INFORMATION. HAS OVER 100 ACTIVITIES COVERING THE ENGLISH LANGUAGE, MATHEMATICS, FRENCH LANGUAGE, GENERAL KNOWLEDGE, GEOGRAPHY AND WORD GAMES. IT COMES WITH A TWO-BUTTON MOUSE TO AID DEXTERITY. THIS IS AN EDUCATIONAL LEARNING COMPUTER DESIGNED TO AID LEARNING THROUGH STIMULATION AND FUN.

LEXIBOOK
Power Academy

When I Grow Up I Want To Be . . .

When I grow up I want to be,
A writer or a poet,
I'd scribble all day,
I'd have my say,
And everyone would know it.

When I grow up I want to be,
A designer for all fashions,
Purple jeans,
Shoe supreme,
You'll love it with a passion.

When I grow up I want to be,
A teacher in a school,
Detentions here,
Scolding there,
I could be so cool.

When I grow up I want to be,
A trainer or a breeder,
Puppies yapping,
The mother napping,
And everyone would meet her.

When I grow up I want to be,
Someone very special,
People's respect,
No one's rejection,
I *will* be exceptional.

Ashleigh Johnston (12)

LEXIBOOK POWER GLOBE
AN EDUCATIONAL COMPUTER TO HELP YOU TRAVEL AND DISCOVER THE WORLD THROUGH A FOUR-VOYAGE DISCOVERY CHALLENGE. INCLUDES MUSIC AND SOUNDS OF THE WORLD, WORLD CULTURES AND CUSTOMS, THE ENVIRONMENT, HISTORY, MONUMENTS, INVENTIONS, GAMES AND FOREIGN LANGUAGES. CHILDREN CAN ALSO ACCESS 32 OTHER EDUCATIONAL ACTIVITIES AND A BONUS ACTIVITY 'THE MISSION' COMBINING PUZZLES, RIDDLES AND QUESTIONS!

I Dream A Dream Of The Future

I dream a dream of the future
That I have a stallion as black as the clear night sky.

Together we will run like the wind
as leaves swirl around our heads.

As they spin we begin to fly
Over the hurdles high in the sky.

We will land on the floor at the finishing line
We'll hear laughing, clapping and cheering,
Oh my!

We will get a medal, a bridle and a free saddle
As well as a purple rosette.

I will be a great flutist playing my tune
In front of three thousand people
It's true!

I will look up above
See spotlights upon me
And handfuls of flowers being thrown from below.

I'll hear humongous applause

A bouquet of flowers will be given to me
by a world-famous musician.

I will love to write poems, scary and funny
They will make you scream and make you laugh.

I will win a major prize.
My poems will be published worldwide.
Nobody knows my name but I will put it on my poems.
And my name will be known by all.

These are my dreams of the future.

Charlotte Glaves (8)

RUNNER UP

LEXIBOOK
The Power Globe

Hopes And Dreams

Every child like me has a hope,
Or a dream, or both, or even a few of eac
That they want to achieve . . .

Some want their chosen profession,
Some want money,
Or even an encounter with a famous celet

I've always wanted to be an author,
The joy of writing stories,
And watching other people reading and admiring your work.

The excitement of seeing your written books,
On sale in shops, alongside the work,
Of your all-time favourite authors.

My entire life I have loved children,
Pretty little babies like my own brother,
He's absolutely gorgeous, his chubby cheeks and enchanting eyes.

My second dream is based on my love of kinds,
And is to work with the cuties in a crèche, aww, how wonderful.
It would be great, seeing their tiny faces, giggling gleefully.

I discovered recently, I like taking photographs,
Getting people to make poses,
And dress up in amazing outfits.

The best place to take photographs is at a wedding,
Asian weddings, all the beautiful, shimmering, glittering garments,
And sparkling gold and silver,
Combined with the world's most precious gems, in a shining necklace.

Every hope, every dream, every wish, every ambition, every plan,
And every goal,
Can be achieved quite simply, and perfectly,
But only if you set your heart to them . . .

I'm trying hard as I possibly can,
To start building the path I will follow in the future, to *my* goal,
And go on, what seems like, a very long journey in my life . . .

Satminder Kaur Reyat (11)

If I Were Rich

If I were rich,
I'd buy a football pitch
I'd also like a swimming pool
I bet my friends would think I'm cool
I'd buy my dad a cool car
He'd drive it to the best bar
That's what I'd do if I were rich.

Jessica Teggart (11)

The Changing Seasons

Summer, autumn, winter, spring,
Now listen to what the seasons bring,
Summer brings fresh fruit and flowers,
Autumn leaves just fall for hours,
Winter's darkness, cold and rain,
Spring, it's time to start again.

Abby Stokes (8)

Doctor

I want to be a doctor
But it may not come true.
I want to help people
And give them the right medicine.
I want to study cells and the
Human body.
What do you want to be when you're
Older?

Manpal Randeva (10)

My Dreams About Gardening

Oh football, oh rugby, oh what a laugh,
Because what calls me is the scrumptious green grass.

The leaf, the flower, the herbaceous bunch,
The fact that you get to make your own lunch.

Oh football, oh rugby, what a load of phewy,
What I like is my own grown apples so chewy.

Adam Phillips (10)

I Wish

I wish to fly up in the sky,
To feel the clouds, to touch up high.
To be as rich as a movie star,
Saving the world or being a pop star.
To fight evil and have super powers,
And always love it for hours and hours.
But what I always wish for, is the world to be safe,
No madness, no bombings.
No killing each other in the streets,
All children in the world are special,
In their own lovely way,
They might be disabled, injured or blind.
But we thrive through the days for all our lives.

Sheun Oshinbolu (11)

Super Hero!

I wish to save the world quite soon,
That is my heroic dream.
I'll save Earth from an alien goon,
And heroic shall I seem.

I will swoop like Spider-Man,
Elegantly saving people like you.
A young hero of supergran,
With eyes of midnight-blue!

I'll arrest burglars for stealing,
Grabbing their hands with glee.
Crawling across the high ceiling,
Just heroic little old me!

I'll save people from fires
Blowing them out with my breath,
Climbing the tall building higher
Saving millions of people from death!

Philippa Tremble (10)

I'll Always Be Winning

I wish I could sit up on high,
To rule both the Earth and sky,
I'd make the world both kind and fair,
And give suffering people food,
That's never there.

I wouldn't waste my time on money,
Because for some people that isn't funny.
While nobody else really cares,
I will never,
Not be there.

I would change the world to a better place,
No one's allowed to have prejudice against race,
I'd cut down pollution,
And I'd think of a solution,
To cancel people's thoughts, of evolution.

But all that will never happen,
I've got to get used to my world,
While people are choking, starving, dying,
In my heart,
I will *always* be winning.

Bryony Potter (11)

My Dream

There's music on the stage
There's music all around
There's flashing lights everywhere
There's cheering all around
Can you guess who they are
Cheering for?

Samantha Meldrum (10)

Vet

I ntelligent

W ary
A nimals are cared for
N icely
T reated for diseases.

T olerant and patient
O r tolerant and kind

B eing aware of animals' feelings
E motions really count

A nimals come first

V ery gentle and kind
E xcellent and skilled
T o help animals.

Elena Ghirardello (9)

Fantasy Land

I've always dreamt of a fantasy land,
where dolphins sing and jump around,
with clouds of foam, the floor is honeycomb,
fudge for trees and bees bring honey just for me,
the snowdrops are made of sugar candy,
the rain is made out of shandy,
on Bonfire Night rockets whistling,
fountains sizzling, the crowd screaming,
waves crashing on the beach,
fish start to get out of reach,
little fairies play with me,
sing, dance and let's be free.
If we all lived in the magic land,
what a world this would be.

Emma Robertson (11)

To Be Or Not To Be

My dream I hope will happen, some day,
somehow, to be or not to be,
a tall ballerina turned into me.

With smooth silky hair and a beautiful face,
long white tights and ballet shoes with a lace.

Dancing in the moonlight, such a wonderful sight,
On my toes with stars so lovely and bright.

I could choose to be rich but money isn't everything,
I could choose to sing and sing.

But no, that is not my wildest dream, or having superpowers,
climbing up a mountain or exploding the two towers.

Ballet is the best
better than the rest.

To be or not to be,
I hope my dream turns out for me.

Laura Hyde (11)

Desert Island Dream

If I lived on a desert island
I'd collect extraordinary shells
I'd pick drum banging coconuts hanging
from palm prickled trees,
and I'd pick exotic fruits like orange and plums.
I'd lay in the starry white sand making ripples
like waves drinking an ice-cold orange cocktail.
I would play with the dolphins swishing
and diving as I'd play.
I would climb the highest mountain on the island
stroking its crusty chipped back.
I'd build a bubbly Caribbean jacuzzi and lay down
on my back dreaming what tomorrow would bring
eating pineapple, pears and grapes,
and singing along with what the desert island makes.

Sian Puckey (10)

The World At Our Feet

Every day you watch the news,
You see death, fights and war.
I just wonder,
Where our morals are,
I feel devastated
What happened to the world
God created
Over which he once elated?
On the news I see
Children just like me,
Living in poor conditions,
Supported by missions,
Animals being hurt,
Houses covered in dust and dirt,
People taunting the old,
Babies abandoned, freezing cold,
People killing with knives and guns,
Children dying in their tonnes.
My dream is this -
To have world peace,
So misery will cease.

Kerry Nesbitt (12)

Saving The World

S aving the world is the best
A lways helping killing demons
V illains beware as the slayer comes
I n the evening when the sun sets
N ot always going straight to the test
G aining full strength.

T o save the world from demons is great
H ell recommended to vampires and all
E arth will be a better place.

W hen the beasts, demons and vampires are all gone
O f all will be well
R oam the nights without a care
L ove the feel of the midnight air
D o all the things you can to

Save the world!

Stephenie Somerton (10)

Saving The World!

When people try to save the world
They think it's really easy,
They pack their bags and head far away
And say, 'It's easy peasy!'

They have a lot of confidence
And they know they're gonna win,
But they're struggling already
And that's before they begin!

So that heart of hope and gracefulness
That was loving, pure and kind,
It's headed off back home again
The challenge twisted his mind!

Now people think it's really hard
And that you have to be really brave,
You have to be strong and tough enough
To walk right over a grave!

But I'll tell you a little secret
Just untangle things all curled,
Recycle and don't litter
That's how to save our world!

Jodie Arnott (11)

The World At Our Feet

Smooth sand under my feet
Palm trees shading me from the sun
Listening to the sea lapping the sand,
Collecting coconuts everyday
Lying in the sun getting brown
Having a dip in the sea
Sleeping in hammocks
The breeze rustling my hair
Sun shining on my back,
Rowing out to sea
Exploring a shipwreck
Digging for treasure
Playing volleyball,
My team wins
Going scuba-diving
Finding different sea creatures in the coral reef
Watching the sea glimmer in the dark,
Beautiful blue cloudless sky
What a beautiful desert island!

Sophie Jones (10)

My Dreams

I'd like to be an actress
or maybe even write,
I'd like to work with animals
but they might scratch and bite.

I'd like to live on my very own island
and even drive a boat.
I'd like to live in a castle
and swim in my moat.

I'd like to become rich
and retire from school
I'd like to live in a mansion
and have my very own pool.

But what I'd most like to be
is plain old normal me.

Kate Thompson (10)

What I Want To Be

When I grow up I want to be great,
When I go to work, I shall say 'hi' to my mate.
I don't want to be in charge of all the mayors,
And I don't want to collect people's bus fares,
But I want to be great!

When I grow up I want to be an astonishment,
But don't want to work for the British Government.
I don't want to be an aerologist,
And I don't want to be a mad geologist,
But I want to be astonishment!

When I grow up I want to be wise
But not someone who tells terrible lies
I don't want to be someone who flies a helicopter,
But I always wanted to be a doctor.

Who is
Great,
An astonishment
And
Who is
Wise.

Christopher Thomas (11)

Orange

Orange are a prowling fox's cunning eyes,
The colour of autumn evening skies,
Beautiful beyond the horizon's line,
The clouds illuminated above the Tyne.
Orange is the burning, blazing sun,
Bathing the world and everyone.
Orange is a tiger full of pride,
Roaming the forests as creatures hide.
Orange is a blanket of crisp autumn leaves,
In which a busy squirrel interweaves.
Orange is the flame from a dragon's tongue,
Until Saint George's victory is won.
The burning is also a feeling inside,
When anger takes over that you want to subside.
Orange is the hair of a comical clown,
Or a beautiful woman on whom it flows down.
Orange is the dying sun in winter,
Orange is the red of a tired painter.
Orange is a colour though often overseen,
By red, yellow, black, gold or green,
That deserves some credit for what it has done,
Brought the world more character and simply . . . fun!

Faye Greason (12)

The Night

As I lay in bed,
Listening to the night's conversations,
And the rain tapping on the window
The moon still hidden with my depression.

I still couldn't sleep
The time I'd spent with her seemed to dissolve away
Only a memory of her was left.
The fuzzy smile and the soft cry.

The room suddenly started to float on top of the moonlight,
Suspense drew over me. 'Could the dead talk to the living?'
Not knowing, yet still thinking, her voice touched my soul
It was true.

She'd never leave without a goodbye,
Her hands parted as a welcome to say goodbye.
I never let go to this day
Her memory will always be.

I woke up with a smile and cuddled up to my teddy bear.
The teddy bear was probably her
Always there for me.

I'll never forget that night.

Kimberley Dakwa (11)

My Dreams

I sit in bed,
And in my head,
I see myself,
In a chair,
In an office,
Falling asleep,
Without a care in the world.

I shut my eyes and dream,
About a desert island,
With a magical horse,
A unicorn perhaps,
But then . . .

The unicorn disappears,
The island disappears,
As a voice shouts -
'Sarah, time for school!'

Sarah Miles (10)

I Could . . .

I could be an explorer and travel round the world,
I could become an author or a cowgirl,
I could be a movie star and earn a lot of money,
I could move to Africa where it would always be sunny,
I could be a sailor and live a life on the sea,
But all I've ever wanted, was just to stay me!

Rachel Bousfield (9)

When I Am Older . . .

When I am older I would like to be
Maybe a teacher, no that's not me!

When I am older and have a family,
Maybe we might go on a jet ski.

When I am older I would like to go
And live on a deserted island where rivers flow.

When I am older maybe I might
Live in a mansion, yeah right!

Emma Beadle (11)

Make The World A Better Place

When I'm walking down the street,
I see the world that's at my feet.
I see dirt and litter, but amongst all this,
bundles of clothes, sleeping bags
with long, sad faces smoking fags,
but people keep on walking by,
it makes me sad, I want to cry.
I want to get them off the street,
get them back onto their feet.
I want to make the world a better place,
I want to put a smile upon their face.

Alice Haguenauer (9)

I Wish

All I wish,
Is to live in my dream,
And stay off school,
Till I'm eighteen.

I would like to be rich,
And never be poor,
A world full of peace,
And not any war.

I'd like to stay young,
And never grow old,
Keep those warm,
Who are always cold.

That's all I wish,
I have to say,
Please make my world,
Like this today.

Emma Hill (10)

The World's At My Feet

Urgh! The Pacific Ocean soaked my trainers!
The world's at my feet
Hastily, I pulled my foot out of the Bermuda Triangle
The world's at my feet.
Ouch! I pricked myself on the Pyramids!
The world was at my feet
I caught my sock on a skyscraper
The world's at my feet.
It's big, but not big enough
The world's at my feet
Earth can't hold me
The world's at my feet
Oh, but the universe is wide
The world's at my feet . . .

Beth Jellicoe (11)

The World At Our Feet

Having super powers would be so cool.
I could fly all the way to school.
Having super powers would be great,
I could make a cake, have a shower,
And still have time for a break.
I wish I had super powers,
It would be the best thing ever.
You never know, I could turn out
Clever!

Ellie Betham (10)

The World At Our Feet

I hope to be a footballer,
Putting balls in the back of the net
Living in a house with millions of floors.

World domination, being the boss
Controlling every nation.

Never going back to school
That will be so cool.

But what if my friends aren't there with me?
Maybe I'll let them in with world domination, maybe.

Sam Peters (10)

The World At Our Feet

If I had lots of money
I would go to Hawaii.

Or I would party
All night and all day.

I might buy an airport
With lots of aeroplanes.

Or I might buy the White House
Or I might stay at home and be me.

I would buy a Ferrari
With 100 litres of fuel.

But it is unlikely
So I will stay at home and be me.

Justin Aunger (9)

I'm In Pop Idol

I went in and got my ticket
I was scared.
Some people were laughing and,
Others crying.
When it was my turn to go,
I was shaking from head to toe.
They told me to come back
The next day.
I came back and sang
With all my heart.
I got in!

Maria Bruce (11)

Super Powers

When I was born I had super powers
It was class,
I was really fast.
I had laser eyes, bullet-proof chest,
Now I fly and save the world.
There was a robbery one day
I had to go and save the day
Once again.

Tiernan Treacy (8)

Super Powers

If I had super powers,
I would meet Bertie Aherne.
I might even live with the Queen.
Hopefully one day,
There will be lots of money waiting for
Me!
There would be a cinema and a shop
Waiting for me and my friends.
All the poor people would be *rich!*
Having my own swimming pool would be great.
Maybe one day I will have super powers.
I hope so, don't you?

Aisling Maguire (9)

The Oscar Day

On the Oscar day
I was so excited
I hoped I would win an Oscar
I had a lovely dress, it was pink
I couldn't wait.

It was finally the moment
'The award for best actress,'
This was the moment I was waiting for
'Goes to Catherine Doherty.'

I was so amazed that I had won
I went up to be awarded my Oscar.
It was golden, heavy and sparkly,
I thanked my mum, dad and my two brothers.
Also my teacher Mrs Clancy.

Then suddenly I woke up, I realised it was only a dream.
Too bad! That would have been really class!

Catherine Doherty (9)

Pop Idol

When I grow up I would like to be on Pop Idol,
Sing, dance and all different things.
I would like to win, win, win.
Singing without the page on the stage,
What a big surprise as I open my eyes,
I have won first prize.
I cry and cry as my singing teacher goes by,
And remember back to when I came,
I wanted to win! Win! Win!

Aoibheann Flanagan (8)

Playing For Man United

Here I am coming onto the pitch.
The game starts with a bit of a twitch.
I take the kick-off.
Arsenal gets the ball,
They're going for a goal.
They miss.
The goalkeeper kicks it out, Ljungberg heads it,
Ryan Giggs gets it, he passes, I pass back,
He goes for a goal, it hits the post.
I get the ball, I shoot, it's a rebound.
I shoot again, it's a goal! Goal! Goal!

My dream come true!

Kieran McGorty (8)

Working With Animals

When I grow up I want to be a vet
So I can help animals with little pink noses,
I love animals, they are so cute!

If there is an animal that is feeling sick
Here I come! Here I come!
I try to make it better
To my delight and surprise I do
I love animals they are so cute!

Rachel Gallagher (8)

My BMW

I can go to 200mph
It has a CD player
It has leather seats
It has trick wheels
It has four pipes
It has sports caps
It has 100 turbo engine.

John Feely (9)

Ferrari

My Ferrari is so fast,
It never comes last.
My friend Barry
Loves my Ferrari,
Because it carries two engines.
CD player, sunroof,
Twin exhausts, great wheels,
Turbo 130 suspension
And alloys!
What more could one ask for?

A dream come true!

Stephen Joseph Maguire (9)

Playing Football For Ireland

When I get older,
I will play for Ireland.
People cheering when I score
People cheering when I score.
People cheering, everywhere.
When I score the people will shout loud!
Loud! Loud! Loud!
A goal!

Nevin McIntyre (8)

The World At Our Feet

I wish I could save the world
And have super powers.
I would leave my mum
Then I'd go and have fun
With my super powers.
I would look around
Above the ground
And put out all the fires.
I would fly with my teddy
And always be ready.
I would help everybody
In the town and beyond.
With my teddy beside me I fly
Then I get home
And I'm always in time for tea.

Kate Coverley (9)

The World At Our Feet

If I became a footballer
I'd score lots of goals.
I'd tackle players that had the ball
And dribble it down the pitch.

Daniel De Niet (9)

The World At Our Feet

If I became rich
I would spend it on myself.
I would buy really nice dresses
For a really special night.
I would go all the way round the world.
I would go to all kinds of different places.
When all the money's gone,
I wouldn't have a clue what to do.
I would look around the garden thinking what to do.
Seeing if there's any more money too.
What if there's not any more.
I will end up very, very poor.

Beth Oxley (9)

The World At Our Feet

I can't wait until I'm famous.
I'll be the main one there.
I'll be like David Beckham
And I'll gloss up my hair.
I'll go up the stage,
I'll be ahead of you.
I'll be number one and you'll be number two.
When I'm going round town
I'll always wear a crown.
Everyone will say, 'There you are,
You wicked, awesome pop star.'
They'll think that you can disappear
And they'll remember the days they used to cheer
Now they just throw money
Clattering is all I hear.

Daniel Meruz (10)

The World At Our Feet

My dream I've always wanted - oh so
I'll really try
To play in a Little League World Series
Oh that would be the life.
Then I'll move on, I will have to be strong.
To play in the Minor League would definitely be wrong.
So I'd have to play in the Majors
Be quick, clever and strong.

But it's all a dream for now and I have to think I might not make the Little League World Series and that would be a stink.

Luke Bayer (10)

The World At Our Feet

I'd like to be an archaeologist
And find lots of things,
Like Howard Carter finding
Tutankhamen's tomb.
I'd like to find Cleopatra
Who was bitten by an asp.
I know a lot about her
Even about her sons.
When I find Cleopatra
I will give her to Ciaro
In a very famous museum.
When I become an archaeologist
I'll find lots of things I will.
So if you want to be an archaeologist
Join me and we'll have a great adventure.

Helena McColl (9)

World At Our Feet

I love going to a party.
One night I went to a party.
The lights went out
I looked around, the Oscars had gone.
I looked out of the window
I saw him take a gun from a guard.
I ran after him, we ran through the park,
The town centre and everywhere else.
When he came to a dead end,
I said, 'Put your hands up,
And put the Oscars in the bag.'
On my mobile phone I rang the police.
They came and arrested him.
I took them back to the party.
I sat down and had lunch.
They gave the Oscars out,
And very surprisingly,
They gave one to me.

Oliver Sapsford (9)

The World At Our Feet

When I'm older I'll be rich.
When I'm older I'll play on a football pitch.
When I'm older I will drive a fast car.
When I'm older I'll own a bar.
When I'm older I'll have lots of fun.
When I'm older I'll have my own gun.
When I'm older I'll have a dog called Jim.
When I'm older I'll have a cat called Tim.
When I'm older I won't have to go to school,
Nope, I'll be swimming in my swimming pool.

Oliver Hunt (10)

World At Our Feet

I would love to be a millionaire
And buy whatever I like.
I would own a giant company
As long as no one goes on strike.

I would drive around in a Ferrari
Then I might go on a safari
I would own lots of houses
And live all over the world.
I would run about and jump and shout
Until I got bored with my money.

Ryan Connolly (11)

Christmas

Winter's coming,
Santa's near,
Jesus' birthday,
Will soon be here.

Christmas crackers,
Lots of toys,
Many presents,
For girls and boys.

Seren Moon (9)

Singing And Winning

I'm the best player for Cardiff City
And I rock and rule,
My friends think it's a pity,
But they all drool.

I'm a pop star that sings a lot,
I sometimes lose the plot,
Yet I'm a striker too,
How about you?

Tesni Phillips (8)

Football Crazy

My name is Sarah and I'm ten years old.
I am quite pretty and my hair's gold.
I'd love to be a footballer,
And wear the colour red.
I play football now
And my manager once said,
'You can be in our team
And follow your dream.'

Two games on and I am still smiling
We lost them both
But hey who's counting,
The season's just started,
And the team are having fun.
The rain has stopped,
Out comes the sun.
The referee gives the whistle a blow
I'm really sorry, but I've got to go.

Sarah Greene (10)

When I Become Rich

When I become rich
I will keep my money
In a shiny gold treasure box.
Sometimes I will give too much money
So you can buy a house.

When I become rich
I would have the best clothes
Full of diamonds and rubies
Shiny as can be.

When I become rich
I would buy
The poshest mansion as big as a whale,
A warm swimming pool just for me.

When I become rich
I would buy
The poshest American car
Which is white as snow.
Would you like to be rich
When you're older?

Freya Hall (8)

When I Grow Up

When I grow up I want to be a footballer.
When I grow up I can score lots of goals I can.
When I grow up I want to be a footballer,
And be as famous as Beckham I can.
When I grow up I want to be a footballer,
And live in a very, very, very big house
With a swimming pool.
I can.

Joshua Woodhall (8)

In The Future

When I'm older I want to . . .
be swimming
swimming in galas
swimming in style.
  I will.

When I'm older I want to . . .
have a costume
with England on the bum
a mermaid in a fifty metre pool.
  I will.

When I'm older I want to . . .
live in a big house
have lots of money.
  I will.

When I'm older I want to . . .
dive into the water
feel the chill down my spine
the water on my fingertips.
  I will.

When I'm older I want to . . .
get a gold for England
feel the excitement of it
Stand on the podium.
  I will.

Eleanor Lord (8)

Saving Animals

When I'm older
I'll go round the world
Saving animals tough and rough
When I'm older.

When I'm older
I'll go in rainforests so noisy
With smell so bad
When I'm older.

When I'm older
I'll save dangerous sharks
Some like great white sharks
When I'm older.

When I'm older
I'll look after dolphins
The prettiest in the pool
When I'm older.

When I'm older
I'll save white rhinos
With all the endangered species of animals
When I'm older.

Stewart Watson (8)

Film Star

When I am older
My ambition is . . .
To be as good as
Steven Spielberg.
I will do that.

When I am older
My ambition is . . .
To be as smartly dressed
As David Beckham.
I will do that.

When I am older
My ambition is . . .
To have a film as
Action-packed as
Mission Impossible!
I will do that.

When I am older
My ambition is . . .
To be as famous
as JK Rowling.
I will do that.

Alex Castle (8)

When I Grow Up I Want To Be . . .

When I grow up
I want to be . . .
A singer on my own
Nervous up on the stage.

When I grow up
I want to be . . .
A famous singer
That everybody meets.

When I grow up
I want to be . . .
A singer up on Fame Academy
Twelve hours a day?

When I grow up
I want to be . . .
A singer and I'm gonna try
To beat the rest
But
To do that I'll have to try my best.
You vote me.

Daisy Riley (8)

Lamborghini

I am in a race.
Red light . . . orange light . . . green light . . . go.
If I lose,
I will bruise . . . my soul.

I am in fifth place.
The engines are furious.
They are raging.
I put on my nitro.
I am in fourth . . . now third . . . now second.
We are still in a race and Dad says, 'It is school time.'

Patrick Mullan (9)

My Dream

Where are all the tigers?
Are they dying out?
I wish I could help them
So now my dream comes out.

I want to fly to India
And get a job there too
I hope I can help them
I hope my dream comes true.

I love their stripy bodies
Their cute little faces
Their long wiry whiskers
Their feet that run the races.

The cubs' little teeth
The adults' big jaws
The cubs' little yelps
The adults' big roars.

I'd really like to meet one
Become its bestest friend
But if you don't help me
They may come to an end.

Olivia Kennaway (9)

Appearing On Pop Idol

Pop Idol! Pop Idol!
How I long to be there.

Oh how great it would be
To sing live on air.

Pete Waterman there with a smile,
On his face.

I stood there in front of him
And sang with such grace.

Dancing would be great
I'd twirl and swirl.

Oh think of the jewellery,
Diamond and pearl.

Lovingly perfect,
Pick me as your pop idol girl!

Chloe Morris (9)

Dreaming

Have you realised that school isn't all?
Sitting there while you could be in Nepal!
You might want to perform on a stage,
Or be President of the United States!
Saving the world from war and suffering,
Being a circus clown, best at juggling,
Or maybe go and join Sherlock Holmes.
Chilling out, chatting on the phone!
You'll be free to do what you want,
Like eat ice creams.
But remember to accomplish those adventurous dreams.

Shilpa Mistry (10)

I've Always Wanted To Be A Singer

I've always wanted to be a singer
With long hair and cool shoes
Jumping up and down on the dance floor,
Showing off all my funky moves.

With all the screaming fans
And making no 1.
Travelling the world
And having the best of fun.

Only you have to be able to sing
And that's the one thing I can't do.
Then again, I can't dance either,
But I love to try, don't you?

Jennifer Speedie (9)

Policewomen

P olicewomen, policemen chase people around
O ver the hills and far away.
L ots of people found
I ndia and Australia
C anada and Greece
E ngland and Florida, coppers all around.
W ith horrible criminals everywhere
O nly the police can handle them
M urders
E verywhere
N ow it's time to end my poem.

See you I'm going.

Rea Swindells (9)

When I'm Rich

When I'm older, I'll be a star
How will I get a car?
Everything in my life is wonderful and good,
Now I'm older, my dreams will hopefully come true.
I'm going to have a kid called Sue,
Me and my kid will live in a mansion,
Ready now I'll never have a tantrum,
I'll be a kid lover,
Collette will have a bed cover,
Hopefully my dreams will come true.

Charley Stott (9)

Aperture Adventure

Click, clack,
Snip, snap.

Develop
Expose

Contact
Lens

Guess who
I am?

Louis Needs (10)

No More War

N ow this fighting has to stop
O r else people will get angry

M any people think war should not happen
O ur world should not be about fighting
R ound the world people are killing each other every day
E veryone should be friends, I think, what about you?

W hy do we have to be this way?
A nd everyone needs to be friends, to make this world a better place.
R espect each other is the way forward.

Scott Edwards (10)

Football Violence

S ome fans are mad
T owards each other
O ver the top they sometimes go
P erhaps we could be friends if we all pull together!

Ross Edwards (9)

Our World

W ashington, Welshpool, Wellington and Wales,
O rlando, Ormskirk, Ottowa and Oslo
R ussia, Rhyl, Ruthin and Rochester
L iverpool, London, Lincoln and Leeds
D enbigh, Denmark, Deeside and Dublin

Our beautiful big wide world.

Josh Davies (9)

The World At Your Feet

When I grow up, I'm going to be
An engineer perhaps, we'll see.
Making robots or things that talk,
Then maybe I could do less work.
Lots of studying and homework will be needed.

So perhaps my teacher should be needed
But then again, maybe not.
Maybe I'll travel to somewhere hot
And stay awhile to enjoy the view,
Then pack my bags and onto somewhere new.

Alex Hooson (10)

The World At Our Feet

I'm lying on some golden sand
Dreaming about being in a band
I'm dying of thirst
It can't get any worse.

I sleep there in pain
You can't hear any crane
I start to feel a tear roll down my cheek
I'm getting really weak
I need something to eat.

I start to get up and search for fresh clear water
I get a bit scared and walk no more,
If only I had some food in store,
I completely collapsed and shouted for help.
I had one last yelp,
I turned red
I was dead.

Eloise Collins (9)

Stranded On A Desert Island

S tranded on a desert island,
T oo far away for any help,
R unning water from the spring,
A nd fish in the sea,
N utritious meat and coconuts,
D elicious fruits from the forest,
E very night the midges gather,
D ancing by the firelight.

O nce I feared the mosquito bites,
N ow I have a strong blanket.

A nd it is made of bracken.

D reaming of being rescued,
E ach day I hunt,
S wim in the sea,
E at my catches,
R est in the shade of the palm trees,
T allest hill from which I watch.

I n case of a ship,
S ailing towards the island,
L uck finally turned my way,
A nd a ship appeared to save me,
N ever again would I leave dry land,
D id I swear when I got home.

Katie Hedgecock (11)

Golden

Watching the sun by the lake,
The soft ripples slowly shake,
She glides across the bluish sky,
Soaring up and soaring high.
Burning beams shine on the street,
Lighting up the bleating sheep.
Reflecting her glow on the golden stream.
The white swans on the waters gleam.
The young birds sleep in their nest,
The older birds fly to the west.
The sun lights up the golden world,
Making the Earth look bright and pearled.

Ciara Hughes (10)

My Dream Of Fame

I tried and tried,
I thought of many ideas,
It happened . . .

I walked into a shop,
I saw a black book,
All new and shiny,
So I picked it up and on it,
Author 'Vaila Whittaker',
I became famous.

I was on Richard and Judy,
I was on CBBC, I even was on
GMTV!
It was wicked and it was easy,
Thinking of adventure or it would,
Be a great fantastic funny one!

Soon I was the richest person of all,
I was fantastic, but soon a new person came out,
She had the looks, the writing and the money,
I had everything one day,
The next I had nothing!

. . . Until my next great idea!

Vaila Whittaker (11)

My Future Dreams

A wedding planner I would love to be,
I would also love to fly over the sea.
America I would love to stay in,
And then I shall not be dim.
My big cousin and brother will come with me,
To fly over the sea.

Australia I would love to go to,
When I am twenty-two
The Barrier Reef looks perfectly peaceful,
And also pretty beautiful.

My other dream is to be,
At the awards of MTV.
I'd meet J-Lo or Blue,
And maybe even kiss their shoe.
Or if not them I'd meet Mis-Teeq,
Now that would be unique.

When I get a car I'd get an Audi TT,
That was made especially for me.
I'd be on the road with my Audi TT,
And then I'd be as happy as I can be!

That's my future dreams,
However spectacular they may seem
They will come true,
When I am twenty-two.
I won't listen to whatever anybody else says,
Because I know that I'll try my best.

Nicolle Gibson (10)

Life In The Future

L ife in the future for me would be to marry Peter Lovenkrands.
I would like to be a beautician when I am older.
F orever, I will always support Glasgow Rangers.
E lephants I want to go see in Africa.

I want to start a business selling rabbits.
N ever smoke or take drugs when I am older.

T he thing I would like to do most, is to be a dancer.
H ope to stay in Australia or Gran Canaries
E xplore the jungle, what an adventure that would be.

F amily is what I want, two boys and a girl.
U ntidy is not how I want to live, I want to be tidy.
T eacher I might do as a part time job.
U nfair I will never be to my family if I have one . . .
R abbits are my favourite animals in the whole wide world.
E xciting is my future life isn't it?

Laura Sweeney (11)

I Hope This Would Never End!

I would live in a golden palace
I would relax in a bubbling jacuzzi
I would exercise in a blooming garden
I would end the day with a bottle of champagne.

I would have a diamond mine
I would laugh at a creative comedy
I would lie in a pit of gold
I would end the day with a party of fame.

I would play with a furry animal
I would chat with a caring friend
I would be loved and cared by my family
I hope this would never end!

Rosie Baggs (10)

Getting A New Pet

Getting a new pet is so much fun, because they are:

G orgeous
E nergetic
T alented
T rusting
I ntelligent
N aughty
G reedy

A dmirable

N oisy
E xcitable
W onderful

P erfect
E njoyable
T hirsty

Pets are all of these things.

Siobhan Dempster (10)

Tropical Fish

On my birthday I will get a tank of tropical fish.
  Scarlet-red fish,
  aqua-blue fish,
  emerald-green fish,
  tangy orange fish,
  golden-yellow fish,
  fuschia-pink fish,
  jazzy purple fish,
  and last but not least,
A small, sleek, shiny, sparkling, silver fish.

Bethan Roberts (9)

A Desert Island

I dream every night about living on a desert island
And this is the way it goes.
The coconuts are brown
And the sun is beating down.
The trees are tall as a house
And the sand is hot.
The sea is blue and
So are you.

Holly Jamieson (9)

What I'd Like To Do

When I grow up
I'd like to be
A vet or something
Like that you see.
I like all animals
Big and small
From tiny mice
To giraffes so tall.

I'd visit the farms to make sheep and cows better.
I'd send them their bills by post in a letter.
I don't think it would always be pleasant you know,
For example when there is frost, rain and snow

Then I would see
Small animals inside
Playful puppies and shy
Kittens try to hide.
I know if I want
This dream to come true
Working hard at school
Is what I must do!

Ashleigh Jackson (10)

My Dream!

My dream is to be an actress
But without all the press.
To stand in front of a camera
And act like Cameron Diaz.
I could act with Leonardo Di Caprio
Even though he would steal the show.
I'll be here and there in every way
I know I'll be tired at the end of the day.

If I'm good I'll be famous
Providing I don't get too much fuss!

Laura Seddon (10)

I Would Like To Be

When I grow up I would like to be an astronaut.
When I grow up I would like to live underground.
When I grow up I would like to have three dogs and a pig.
When I grow up I would like to save the tigers.
When I grow up I would like to live in Florida.
When I grow up I would like to travel the world.

Jamie Dreiling (9)

Friends And Family

Do you have a friend who's always by your side?
Do you have a friend who makes you warm inside?
Do you have a friend who helps you on your way
And buys you sweets and presents when you can't afford to pay?

Do you have a brother who shouts and yells all day?
Do you have a brother who always wants to play?
Do you have a brother who runs as fast as you?
Because he tied your shoes together, and covered them with glue!

Do you have a daddy who picks you up from school?
Do you have a daddy who sometimes plays the fool?
Do you have a daddy who's always very happy?
Except when it's late at night and he's changing the baby's nappy!

Do you have a mummy who's always full of love?
Do you have a mummy who's an angel from above?
Do you have a mummy who next week goes to China
To make money for sick people by walking the Great Wall of China?

Gethin Lawrence (9)

My Wish

I wish I had a playful puppy,
I'd name him Lucky.
He would be a Labrador,
I'd teach him to open the door.
He would be small and black,
And would eat everyone's snack.
To get my wish, I'll have to work hard on my dad,
He says having a puppy is bad.
Too much to do, too many walks.
I'd like that. It would give me time for a talk.
I'd stroke him every day,
And let him have a really good play.
Never mind, when I'm older,
Maybe my dad will get bolder.
If not, when I leave home,
I'll get my puppy so I won't be alone.

Carys Truelove (10)

A Whole World Ahead Of Me

I've got a whole world ahead of me,
I could travel around the world,
Discover many countries,
See all the sights there are to see.

I could even become a vet
Working among all the animals.
Maybe I could become a TV presenter,
Flying to countries by jet!

What about an author,
I could write stories and poems galore
Publish all my masterpieces,
Then go and write some more!

I have dreams of being a violinist,
And play for the world to hear.
I could play in a huge orchestra,
So confident, not full of fear.

I could even be in the Olympics!
Using my gymnastics skills.
Jumping off the vaulting horse,
Running and jumping for miles!

These are my dreams what I want to be,
My ambitions and hopes what I want to see.
Travelling to places flying over sea,
Because I've got a whole world
Ahead of me.

Laura Macintosh (10)

I Wish . . .

I wish I never had to go to school
I wish I had a swimming pool,
I wish I was a millionaire
I wish I had a grizzly bear
I wish I could fly
High in the sky
I wish I was a better footballer
I wish I was a few inches taller.
I wish I played for Man United
I wish I did something so I would get knighted.
I wish my front teeth were straighter
I wish I was on the football team and not a spectator.
I wish that I could be immortal
I wish I had a real live turtle
I wish I had a dinosaur
I wish I could end world war.
I wish I was a deep-sea diver
I could explore the sea and find a fiver.
I wish . . . I wish . . . I wish . . .

Gurpreet Johl (9)

Living On A Desert Island

No food, no rain.
Just sunlight streaming down.
Living on a desert island, my worst nightmare.
The sea sways silently on.
People scavenging for food, as the sun blazes down.
What are we going to do?
It is just a nightmare.
Living on a desert island is a living hell,
Wishing it was all a bad dream.
It was all torment and torture.
Living on a desert island, my worst nightmare . . .

Omobolaji Oladipo (10)

I Dream

I dream of flying
I dream of swimming with dolphins
I dream of having super powers
I dream of making my sister happy
I dream of buying my dad a bike
I dream of having a puppy
I dream of flying.

Paige Hempsall (7)

Stranded!

I'm stranded on an island
I don't know where to go,
There's nothing in my stomach,
My water's running low.

I want to see my family,
I want to see my friend,
On this desert island,
I'm going round the bend!

Finally, a rescue boat,
It's come to rescue me,
Oh my word, what are they doing!
They're going back out to sea!

Katy Williams (9)

The Way My World Is

I wish I could fly through the skies of blue,
Over land and sea, through the land that grew.

I dream of the impossible, someone that I adore,
Someone that I love who has gone,
To come running through the door.

I imagine things that could be real,
But disappear when I reach out to feel.

I see things happen before these very eyes,
Flashing through my mind, some things stay, some things die.

I sense things happen, people near,
Making me happy, or filling me with fear.

I feel pleasure or pure pain,
I can choose to lose or gain.

I hope to be successful in the future,
And in the present,
I hope the world would quit the fighting
And be a bit more pleasant.

I can't choose the way I look,
I can't choose the way I sound,
But why don't you stop and imagine,
Now what have you found?

Madison Clare (12)

Dreams And More Dreams

I've had so many dreams over the years
I would stand in the theatre and everybody would cheer.
My second dream is to be a great vet,
So I can look after all the cute pets.
Plenty of cuddles, plenty of strokes,
Plenty of noises coming out of all their throats.
So I'll leave it there but there's still so much more to say.
You never know I could be a lifeguard watching over the bay one day.

Emma Cass (9)

The World At My Feet

Teachers, doctors, nurses,
Which do I want to be?
If the world was at my feet
I could be any!

Actress, singer, dancer,
The list can never end.
Or just work in the post office
And letters I would send.

So many occupations,
So many years to come.
For now I'll stick to homework
Whilst I chew this piece of gum.

Let's keep on dreaming!

Natalie Bagwell (11)

Jesus

Jesus is our life,
Jesus is our might,
But he wouldn't let you fight,
Jesus is our friend,
Jesus is the Lord,
Jesus is the one,
Jesus is the chosen one,
He shall lead us to victory,
The only thing we owe Jesus is our souls and our lives.
Jesus is an honest man,
He will give up his life for you but would you

do the same?
Jesus is the bravest man I know,
He stopped the Romans from invading,
His life was unspared,
Because he tried to free me and you.

Balvinder Singhru (10)

The World At My Feet

Maybe I'll be a vet
And heal animals' cuts.
Or maybe a kennel assistant
And take care of helpless mutts.

Maybe I'll be a doctor,
And take care of little ones
Or I could work in smokers' helplines
And save people's lungs.

Maybe I'll be an astronaut
And fly to the moon.
Maybe I'll be the President
I'm thinking far too soon.

What job will I do?
And where does it and me meet?
I'm lucky to be a kid,
Because the world is at my feet.

Louise Anderson (11)

Super Powers

If I could have some super powers,
That would be so great,
But please don't ruin my destiny,
And also not my fate.

I could fly with laser eyes,
And be bulletproof through and through.
If I keep on hoping,
It maybe will come true.

If I were a superhero,
I could be so strong.
I could hold a heavy, tall building
Maybe the Parthenon!

If I could have super powers,
That would be so great
But at the moment I'm just a schoolgirl,
So I just dream it's my fate.

Jessica Dyer (10)

I Want To Be A Criminal Catcher

I can fly as fast as a shooting star,
I can pick up an elephant and throw it far,
Safeguarding the skies,
Making sure no one dies,
I am the Criminal Catcher!

Got my powers from a lab disaster,
Of superheroes I am the master,
I have myself only
Boy, am I lonely but,
I am the Criminal Catcher!

Ben Phillips (9)

Dad's Ferrari

Dad's Ferrari, sleek and red,
On the race track always ahead.
Only one owner, in concours condition,
Rear wheel drive and five speed transmission.

Dad's Ferrari, wild and fast
Watch that speedometer as it flashes past.
Into the tiny door, he heads for the hills,
He zooms off changing gears, it's such a thrill.

It sits next to a Jaguar, the BMW and the Lotus.
My dad he has a load of motors.
If they're racing on the track,
Most of them, they won't come back.

Dad's Ferrari is not what it seems,
Because it's always in his dreams.
Me, I think it's great fun,
When I grow up, I might have one!

Theo Tipping (8)

When I Grow Up I Want To Be . . .

A girl with a house made of money
And a bowl full of honey.
I wish I had blonde hair to go everywhere.
I want to be a polar bear
To live in the snow.
Where flowers they grow
I wish I was a bubble to fly everywhere
When someone pops me I go everywhere.

Megan Bell (7)

What I Would Like To Be

When I grow up I'd be a wacky scientist
Smart as can be.
I'd sleep and drink science
And live under the sea.
I'd always make a mess,
I'd be a picky chooser saying no or yes.

Jordan Horne (8)

The Army

I'm going to be in the army
Oh ye, oh ye

I'm going to be the best
Oh ye, oh ye

I'm going to save the world
Oh ye, oh ye

I'm going to fight evil
Oh ye, oh ye

The world is saved.
Oh ye, oh ye.

David Collins (9)

World To Decide

If you were to help one person,
Who would you pick?
Maybe someone popular or with special needs,
Could be a sports star,
Or anything,
For you to decide.

If you were to buy one thing,
What would you buy?
Maybe something cheap or expensive,
Something big or small,
Or anything,
For you to decide.

If you could stop one fight,
Would you know what to stop?
Maybe a war or a wrestling match,
Or anything,
For you to decide.

If we could pick what we wanted to be,
What could we be?
Maybe a teacher or a doctor,
Could be receptionists,
Or anything,
For ourselves to decide.

Susie Clark (10)

Superhero

I've dreamed of having super powers
I've thought of flying high
I've talked about my biggest dream
To soar right through the sky.

If I was a superhero
I'd save the world each day
From earthquakes, meteors and tidal waves
It would always go my way.

In Greece there is a landslide
There's a fierce storm in France
There are huge hailstones in Italy
But I'd give them all a chance.

I'd help injured creatures
Make evil turn to good
Make people who treat others badly
Treat them how they should.

I know it's just another dream
That I've finally got through
But maybe when I'm older
It really might come true.

Charlie Steer (10)

Tomorrow

Tomorrow I shall see the shining stars,
The whirling galaxy and dusty Mars.

Tomorrow I will sail the Nile
And try to decode the Sphinx's smile.

Tomorrow I will whizz back in time,
To greet the dinosaurs and witness the dawn of time.

Tomorrow I shall explore the mysterious sea,
Swim with magical dolphins and hear them sing to me.

Tomorrow I shall fly like a free bird,
Soaring over oceans and smiling at the world.

Today, I just woke up,
And guess what - it's already tomorrow!

Geila Alpion (11)

Octopus Stew

Oh, octopus stew,
I'd look ready for you
I dearly adore you
Oh truly I do!
You're smashing to see
And tasty to chew
You slide down my belly
Saying 'Hullabaloo.'

You're slimy, you're chewy
You smell like shampoo
You twirl round inside
With puddles of goo
Yet I would glue pasta
And salt on my shoe
For one tasty spoonful
Of octopus stew!

Junior Wamba (9)

Future

Future may be out of sight
You cannot reach it and hold it tight.

Men have found and used oil,
From deep down in the soil.
But have we thought carefully like rain,
In the future what we shall gain?

Earthquakes shook forever's worth,
Climate warming hits the Earth.

We thank Thomas Edison for giving us light,
Making the world beautifully bright.
But have we ever thought the future enough,
That changing back would be ever so tough?

Polluted air circled around us,
Lack of electricity makes streets clamorous.

My hope for the rest of my days,
Is that Earth would not pollute any kinds of ways.
For future may be out of sight,
But you can hold it tight.

Mimi Leung (11)

Travelling With Hamish

Elephants are my favourite animals,
So I'd love to bathe with one I'd call
Hamish Smith.
We'd do everything together,
Even if it was miserable weather.
First we'd see the Eiffel Tower,
Oh my God the sun turned into a shower!
Hamish's favourite bun is a Danish pastry.
Mmmm . . . that's it, we'll go to Denmark and see

Copenhagen.
The weather's a bit dull, we'd better hurry.
We'll go to China to see the great wall,
And together we'll share a Thai chicken curry.
Last but not least,
We'll go and scuba dive on the great Barrier Reef.
Oh wow! Look at that rainbowfish,
Now that sea horse, golly that's a huge crab.
Oh no look at the time! Mum will be worried,
I was only supposed to go to the corner shop!

Holly Smith (11)

An Exciting Holiday

An exciting holiday I would love,
I would stare up at the sky above,
I would get my toast and put on some honey,
I would go into town and spend lots of money.
Then I'd come home and see all my friends,
I'd tell them the story that never ends.

Melanie Sanders (11)

The World

The sea is blue,
The land is green,
What a wonderful place
The world has been.

But now the world
Is covered in dirt,
Tears and holes,
Just like an old shirt.

Though, if you and me,
We work together,
The world could be happy,
Forever and . . .
Ever.

Miranda Bane (11)

I Want

I want to be a doctor,
Because I want to help people live.
I want a dog of my very own,
Because I would like to take it for walks.
I want to swim with dolphins,
Because they are my favourite underwater

creatures.
I want a chocolate maker,
Because I love chocolate.
I want to make nice dreams come true,
Because I want to make people happy.
I want to meet a tooth fairy,
Because I could ask where my teeth are.
I want
I want
I want.

Bethan Ferguson *(7)*

Flying

If I could fly,
Like a bird in the sky,
I'd take off from the floor,
I'd swoop and soar,
Over the treetops,
Below the clouds,
I'd wave down at the
Cheering crowds,
Above the shoppers,
Looking down on the cars,
At night I'm amongst
The twinkling stars,
When I land
Back on the ground,
The sound of applause
Rings all around,
I take off again,
And form a loop-the-loop,
Once again crowds
Cheer and whoop,
I land again
Bow and twirl,
I am the amazing
Flying girl!

Jemma Mobbs (10)

Saving Farm Animals

Rusty roofs repainted grassy green,
Muddy fields transformed into colourful meadows.
Rumbling tractors fall silent,
Buzzing bees bob among grazing cows.
Fiery nitrates melt away,
Feel the warm fluffiness of an old ewe.
Change is good,
A farm becomes a sanctuary.

Anna Eunson (11)

My Dreams

I want to be a scientist, the very, very best,
Helping people, saving lives and doing all the rest.
Discovering cures for diseases and things,
The thoughts will come into my head with little pings.

Making gadgets for a mission to Mars,
Inventing giant flying cars.
Holograms, teleporters, the works,
Saving everybody from the super disease that lurks.

Being on television with my infrared vision,
Using computers to make the ultimate decision.
Discovering a new type of gravity,
Helping people live fathoms beneath the sea.

A perfect device I will invent all shiny and new,
Maybe even a robot, but only just a few.
Making electric hats that keep the time,
A new type of camera for fighting crime.

So where will we be in the next century?
We might even be living on Mercury!
So I want to be a scientist, the very, very best,
Helping people, saving lives and doing all the rest.

Aled Jones (10)

SOS Ourselves

With all the evil in the world,
To the ground our health is hurled.
With all the love we cherish and keep,
While others merely perish in sleep.
We are all priceless works of art,
Our price comes from the heart.
Friends and family crawl from the dim,
Others in their sorrow swim.
So hold forever onto hope,
Wash away the misery with soul happy soup.
Friends forever,
Stay together,
SOS ourselves.

Zoe Mackey (10)

Designer Dream

So, your question is what I'd like to be?
A designer of course, it's not hard to see.
I will design for an actress, an actor, a king
I will design for a pop star that can really sing
I will design all fish's tails that live down in the sea
And the mermaids and mermen for they recommend me.
I will set up a mall that sells all my hip stuff,
All pink, red and shiny, brand new and so lush.
And I will design for a princess lots of glittery things
All wrapped up in paper and tied up in strings.
I will design leather sofas and bed covers too
And they will be all for sale for me and for you.

But I am still young and it's dreams in my head
That I think of in day and when I'm comfy in bed.

Harriet Beth Ainsley Carr (10)

Living On A Desert Island

D oing nothing at all
E very day chilling out
S itting on a sandy beach
E verywhere so quiet
R eading books in lonely places
T ired all the time.

I sn't it a lovely place?
S ilent where I sit
L isten to the birds and animals
A cross the seas and rivers
N othing to do at all except
D rinking lots of water.

Amy Ball (10)

When I Get Older . . .

When I get older I want to learn how to fly,
Up and up soaring into the sky.
When I get older I'll learn how to see,
Through walls and ceilings and even a tree!
And when I get older I'll learn how to write,
So fast that 3,000 pages will only take one day and one night.
When I get older, I'll learn to walk through walls,
Out from the kitchen and into the hall.
And when I get older I'll become a . . .
Superhero!

Richard Beck (10)

My Secret Dream

My secret dream, I dream every night
Is one, to fly as high as a kite!
Two, is clear,
I'll make items fly here, then disappear!
Three, with half a spin, and a little grin,
I'll find myself my perfect twin!

Four,
Just to add to it all,
With cash, from me, I'll make it pour!
Five, to make me quick to arrive,
I'll grab my motorbike and off I'll drive!
But most of all to please all mothers,
I'll be filmed giving hands, and helping others.

Lisa Black (11)

My Dream

I dream of designing clothes
Which will be worn in groves
I'd think of a brand name like *Star*
While driving around in my car.

The clothes I design for people
Will be easy to see from a steeple
The clothes I design will be so bright
They'll be so easy to spot at night.

I'll have a whole group of friends
To help out on my loose ends
One of their names will be
Anita M Lee.

I'll live in Canada when I'm older
Although in winter it will be colder
Daisy and Lily will be my kids
I'll buy them make up for their eyelids.

Rosie Cochrane (9)

What I Should Be

When I was in school the teacher gave us a kind of test
She said, 'I want to know what you want to be when you grow up the best.'
So I thought and thought and thought,
It would be cool to be a robber but what if you got caught?
I could be a basketballer, I'm actually pretty good,
But I think people like that are snobby and rude.
I could be a teacher but that would be boring
Or I could be a pilot soaring and soaring.

I could be an electrician but what if you got electrocuted?
Nah, I don't think me and electricity are quite suited.
I could be a waitress serving out food
But when it comes to balancing trays I'm no good.
I could be a maid serving a rich family
But what if I was late, would they react calmly?

So I said to the teacher, 'What can I write?'
Some people want to fight crime at night.
Others want to be lawyers and stuff.
I don't know what I want to be but I'm troubled enough.
People always saying you're growing up and have to go to schools
Because you don't want to be like your dad working with tools.
Just leave me alone leave me be
And when I'm eighteen, I might want a job that I see.

Shannon Lawson (10)

In The Future

I might like to dance like a pop star,
I might like to be a scientist,
I might like to be an artist,
Or I might like to be a writer.
Whatever I am of one of these,
I hope happy memories come to me.

Suzannah Vincent (8)

Autumn

Descending leaves fall to the ground,
Twirling, twisting, round and round,
Autumn season is almost here,
The smell of freshness is oh so near.

The crisp, cool breeze
Shakes the leaves from the trees,
Autumn takes away the green,
Golden-bronze and brown is all that can be seen.

Ryan Larkin (10)

Around The World

When I grow up I want to explore the world.
I'll take a fast boat to St Petersburg.
I'll explore the mountains looking for snow tigers,
And capture one to bring home.
Next I'll go to the Antarctic and I'll go to Australia on the way.
I'll swim with the sharks.
It will be hot but I'll have to wrap up for the Antarctic.
I'll have to dodge the penguins
I'll catch a whaling boat to South America.
We'll be followed by a school of dolphins.
I'll fly in a plane above the Andes
I'll take Concorde back to Britain.

Jake W Taylor (9)

Pop Idol

P op singers sing their songs,
O n to the judges
P eople want to be pop stars.

I n the next round
D rinking water
O n their way to the judges
L ike everybody to think they are good.

Rebecca Plank (10)

My Wonder World

Wouldn't it be great without any war?
That's in my imaginary world,
That's what I saw.
There is no real reason
But it still carries on.

Wouldn't it be great without any crime?
Nothing gets stolen,
No wasting of time,
People would live in harmony,
People would all be friends.

Without things bad,
Wouldn't it be great?
There would be friendships to be had,
But no hate.

Wouldn't it be great without any war?
That's in my imaginary world,
That's what I saw.

Jennie Hockey (11)

My Dreams And Wishes

Dreams and wishes
I have loads.
One to write
Of fairies and toads,
I wish to be an author!

Another one is
For success.
A decent job,
A life not a mess,
I wish for good money!

This is for the world:
Wars to stop,
Dying end,
To keep every treetop.
I wish for world peace.

But most of all,
I hope for
Laughter,
Smiles and more,
I wish for a happy future!

Sarah Hocking (10)

The World Was At My Feet

One day I went to the Oscars,
To see if I had won,
I waited, waited and waited,
But no luck.
I thought my luck was done,
I heard my name clearly,
Surprise, shock galore,
Make believe, dream or reality.
Pinch, pinch, oh that was sore!
I stood up and started walking the long, red rug.
I bowed to all the applause,
Until I reached the stand,
I accepted my trophy,
And took the microphone.
Staring at the people,
My mouth went dry and numb,
I started my acceptance,
It didn't feel so bad,
I realised in a second,
The world was at my feet.

Jessica Heffer (9)

Making A Difference To Life

What else would I want?
Helping people, making things better and best of all for me.

Stopping time, that's the thing!
The thing that can change everything.

Not only that, but to go back in time too,
Which will get rid of the bad things that I still do.

I want to look at what I did,
What was wrong that affected me like this?

I might have done something wrong,
Something wrong that I can now change for good.

It will reshape my life totally,
Making a huge difference to me.

If only I can do it,
Do the things that will transform my life.

If . . . If only I can do it . . .

Abida Rahimi (10)

Animal Friends

A nimals are my best friends,
N ever let them down,
I always wanted to work with them
M ammals and fish and even reptiles,
A nimals like everyone who likes them too,
L ove them and care for them, just as I do.

F un, frisky and full of energy
R unning and jumping up at you,
I think they're cute when they're asleep
E nergetic and love to play
N ever tease them they hate that,
D ogs are my favourite of them all,
S ave the animals or suffer the lot.

Nicole Ball (10)

My Kite

Soaring
High above my head.
You will see my marvellous kite.
I designed it all by myself you see.
I used really colourful paper.
I assembled the frame in wood.
And I painted it in
Lovely
Colours.

Rebecca Kirk (9)

When I Am A Superhero

When I am a superhero,
I will glide,
Across the sky,
I'll fight all the baddies,
And save people from burning towers.

When I am a superhero,
I will fight the wrong,
I'll save the right,
I'll track down robbers and help the police.

When I am a superhero,
I will glide across the sky,
I'll watch out down below,
And stop the world from being nasty to each other.

Emily Jones (8)

My Future

When I am older,
I want to be
A poet who writes poems,
A lot more than three!
Poems are great,
Don't you see.
Poems about animals, people and me!
I would write things like
How I want to be a poet
So now you will know
How my future
Will be.

Zoe Yates (9)

The World To Me!

I wake up and I'm in a cage!
There's no way out.
Phew, Mummy's here and she lifts me out.
That's better, I can crawl about!
I'm off on an adventure,
I'm off to the wood,
Mummy likes to sit on the trees,
Especially when she's having food.
Argh! A monster,
It's chasing me, it's chasing me!
I'm safe, Mummy's clicked it off,
And now she's gone to make a cup of tea.
Oh no she's not,
She's going to the magic place
Where din-dins goes in cold
And comes out hot, it's ace!
What's that funny box?
With little people inside?
Daddy likes to watch it,
And he watches it with pride!
What's that window with a baby in like me,
And a Mummy like my mummy,
And people like my family?
Oh and that baby's got another dummy.
What's that sun
That you switch off and on?
Sometimes it's bright then,
Other times it's gone.
This is today's world,
What will tomorrow bring?

Jessica Nightingale (10)

Dove

I'd send a dove with love
To the one that I really love
He'd send one back with a great big sack,
So I'm sure he's the one that I love.

He said he had been to see the Queen,
He went last night at 8.15.
He said that she said he'd been and seen
But I still can't believe he's met the Queen.

Our love is like a circle that never ever ends
I think it's true, it's up to you
Is it over or what then?

Of course it's not, you stupid thing,
What made you think of such a thing?
I do not know
But I love you.

Siobhan Tomlin (11)

My Dream

I want to be courageous
And head of my embassy.
I want to have people look up to me,
And think I'm a hero.

I want to travel the world
And make a difference to those
Who are less fortunate,
Make them see the meaning of life
And what it's worth.

I want to bring back antiquities
Like Indiana Jones,
Be chased about by the Nazis
In a huge tank chase.

I become a lawyer and emigrate to America,
Be rich and have a huge apartment.
Be an art collector and paint pictures.

I have a huge row of cars:
Two Ferraris, BMW, Mercedes, Jaguar, Limo.
Two motorbikes, a helicopter and my own private jet.

I grow old, married with four children,
Two boys, and two girls.
Fourteen grandchildren, all running around me.
I want to always write stories and poems
About my life.

I die with my name in the history books,
And a palace up in Heaven.

Jessica Russell (11)

My Dream!

I hip hopped onto the stage,
There I sang a long page
At the end I heard a long applause
After I walked through the doors.
I felt like I was flying through the clouds
Up, up high into the sky.
It was so cold I thought I would cry.
Then all of a sudden I felt a bump on my head.
I woke and found myself tucked up in my bed.

Charlotte Pascoe (11)

A Dream About Animals

Crafty crocodiles
Slithering snakes
Tiny tigers
Arguing apes

Giant giraffes
Munching mice
Hurrying horses
Leaping lice.

Emily Wilkins (10)

Hero From Space

Astie the astronaut has come from outer space
Astie the astronaut will save the human race
She's whizzing down from Mars
Past the rockets and the stars
To kick that meteor very far.

So Astie the astronaut is back in outer space,
Astie the astronaut has saved the human race.
She's whizzing back to Mars past the planets
And space cars.
Will we ever see that astronaut again?

Harriet Conner (10)

Patches

Tickly whiskers
Cute little nose
Paws yellow
Paws on my chest
Little lop ears
Burrows in the hay
Eats carrots
Climbs on the wood
Thumps when annoyed
I love Patches
When I become a vet
I will have loads of little rabbits.

Rachael Farquharson (9)

Winning Crufts

Walking round the show ring, my dog and I,
Look at the owners, they seem rather sly,
My dog walks up and down regally like a queen,
I feel so proud, she's the best she's ever been.
Corpulent corgis go trotting on last,
Following batty beagles who are going fast.
The canine parade is all shapes and sizes,
All hoping to win some glittering prizes.
The aristocratic Alsations look down their noses,
Whilst my English setter goes through her poses.
Next we have to do an agility course,
She jumps gracefully like a champion horse.
Next we all stand up in a line,
The judges confer, they are taking their time.
Third is snotty Miss Amanda Harness,
Leading the dog Midnight Darkness,
Second is soppy spaniel, Rusty Iron,
Led by his owner, Miss Anna Frion.
I cross my fingers and hope to win,
They call out my name above all the din.
My dog wags her tail and starts jumping up,
As I am handed the big shining cup.
All I can hear is the roar of the crowd,
The clicking of cameras is really quite loud.
I have had so much fun on this brilliant day,
I am so happy I don't know what to say!

Rebecca Roddan (9)

My Wish

My wish is to become a choreographer

If I was a choreographer,
I would shout so loud
I would bounce on my bed,
I would be very proud,
I would hold on to my favourite ted.

If I was a choreographer
I would sing with glee
I would buy new shoes
I would shout, *'Yippee*!'
That's what I will do if my wish came true!

Kashika Paris (10)

The Mountain Peak

When I'm at the mountain peak,
first I see crevasses deep.

Then I see the blazing sun,
which makes me want to have some fun.

Slipping, sliding on the snow,
taking care of how I go.

It's very peaceful here today,
how I wish that I could stay.

High above the treetops and,
high above the birds on land.

Being here is such a treat,
with the *whole* world at my feet.

Amy Kerslake (9)

Pit Stop

The lights come on,
And I set off down the track.
Up the straight, and round the curve,
And through the pits and out again.
I came down the slope,
And across the finish line.

Neil Marshall (10)

What I Would Like To Be When I Grow Up

I'd like to be a clown and walk upside down,
And wear pyjamas and slip on bananas.
I'd play with bears, put them in pairs.
I'll stroke the cats while they are asleep
On the mats
And trick and pick the flowers.

I would juggle with balls
Make lots of trouble,
Blow bubbles and stand in puddles.

Ashleigh McNaughton *(8)*

I Want To Become

I want to become a writer,
With poems, stories and books,
Maybe a novel with love and romance,
Flowers and chocolates and a trip to France.

A thriller with robbers and crooks,
Actors and actresses those with good looks.
Bringing alive scenes from the pages of my books.

My picture in all of the papers,
A millionaire would be great,
And maybe one day with a dream in my mind,
I would have J K Rowling as my best mate.

We would swap ideas and make lots of notes,
It's getting late now time for our coats.
Back to reality, down to Earth with a bump,
Best finish my homework now before I get a thump.

Leanne Boycott (10)

My Time On Pop Idol

If I was on Pop Idol, and I sang with my heart,
Everything in my body starts to shake and my nerves start.
Poetry and singing is my favourite thing,
But all I want to do is sing and sing.

In Pop Idol I'm scared if I forget the lines,
I'll practise and practise till it's been a thousand times.
I'll sing and sing with all my might,
Until it becomes midnight.

As soon as I sing,
With my good luck ring, I stretch one note high.
My singing is well,
I think it went swell, I hope it's time for goodbye.

Now it's time for the comments of my song,
I hope it went well and it didn't go wrong.
Will they say it was good? Will they say it was bad,
Or will they say it was completely sad?

They said it was the best,
Out of the rest,
And thought I should enter the singing contest.
I'm through!

Farah Laskar (9)

What Shall I Be?

When I grow up what shall I be?
Will I be a sailor who journeys the sea?
A student who studies the law?
No, to me those things sound a bore.

Then, what shall I be?
A teacher, a doctor, or maybe a cook?
No, they don't seem the ones for me!

Oh! What shall I be?
I've gone through all the lists.

Oh, what shall I be?
Well, now I think, we'll just have to wait
And see!

Porshia Athow (10)

Teacher

A senior school teacher,
Is what I want to be,
Teaching history day after day
That's the job for me.

Head of my department,
And deputy of the school.
Head of the Year 7s
All the pupils think I'm cool.

From Cleopatra to Hitler,
I'll show them what's what.
Saxons, Romans, Celts,
We'll study the whole lot.

I'll make my lessons fun
And interactive too.
School trips to Warwick Castle,
And other places too.

Robert King (10)

My Dog Jake

He walks out the door very slow,
For no one knows where he will go.
He walks as slow as a moving snail,
Gently wagging his beautiful tail.
When he got out he started to run,
As fast as a bullet getting shot out a gun.
Jake ran on the road, he got knocked down,
That's why we had to put him down.

He's now in Heaven,
Really livin',
Chasing his ball around.

Jennifer Cardigan (11)

My Wonderful World

In my wonderful world,
There is peace and joy,
Happiness not sorrow,
And no one knows how to cry.

In my wonderful world,
Every child has toys and books,
Love and affection,
And nobody cares about looks.

In my wonderful world,
Selfishness is against the law,
There is no petrol polluting the air,
And of happiness there is a lot more.

In my wonderful world,
Dreams all come true,
No nightmares are needed,
And there is a place for me and you.

Wendy Bold (10)

Children Of The Future

We are the children of the future,
The world is at our feet.
Strangers will walk hand in hand,
Glad that they did meet.

What you teach your children now,
Will make Earth a better place.
No more children dying,
No more punching in the face.

We will stop the wars,
And let good reign.
Get rid of petty fighting,
Banish hurt and pain.

This is my goal in life
And one day you will hear,
Of Prime Minister, Annie Beverley,
Destroying hurt and fear.

Annie Beverley (10)

I Wish I Had Super Powers

I wish I had super powers,
How fun it would be,
I could fly in the sky and everything will I see,
I will be able to pick up chairs and fight the bears,
They'll be so afraid of me,
I could turn the rain to sun,
The hard work to fun,
I could fly through the stars,
Until I get to Mars,
I'll get rid of all that's bad,
And no one would ever be sad.
Oh! I wish I had super powers!

Bethany Williams (8)

The Platy-Roo

We had been sailing for ninety days now
Hoping to find a new island somehow
Our food had started to run low
We were running out of petrol, the pace was slow
I was sitting and eating my last piece of bread
When a voice shouted 'Land straight ahead'
I rushed out onto the rusty metal deck
There it lay, a minute green speck
The next day we finally reached it by daybreak
'Water!' shouted one of my men, we saw a shimmering green lake
We all tumbled out on a warm sandy bay
'I'll call it Salvation Island,' I said without delay
We all kneeled at the lake and drank our fill
I looked up, I could have sworn I saw a yellow bill
It disappeared quickly in the undergrowth
To find it again was my solemn oath
We walked through colourful jungles and up a steep slope
Mosquitoes bit us, it was hard to cope
Then we started to go back to the ship
I was so disappointed, I bit my lip
I bent down to tie my muddy shoe
Then I saw it in the grass: a duck-billed Platy-roo
The Platy-roo has two springy brown feet
He only eats Salvation Island wheat
He is only six inches tall
And can jump over a two metre wall
Of all the places I have been
And all the animals I have seen
I will always savour it
The Platy-roo is my favourite.

Joram D Los (10)

My Dream

I dream of being a superstar,
Because I want to be popular.

I dream of being a little star,
Because it shines so far.

I dream of having a lovely flower,
Because it has wonderful power.

I dream of travelling to lots of places,
So I can meet lots of new faces.

I dream of having nice clothes,
So I can pick the one that I chose.

I dream of having the beauty,
Because I am so cutie.

I dream of winning the lottery,
Because it's my priority.

I dream of being a princess,
Because I am simply the best.

Sanya Sacranie (9)

What I Would Like To Be

When I grow up I would like to be
A ballerina girl who will spin around and touch the ground.
When I tiptoe I'd touch my hip.

Rebecca Cartlidge (8)

What I Would Like To Be

I would like to be an author and write lots of magic stories.
When I grow up I would like to be a ballerina and walk across
the stage and wriggle my bottom.
When I grow up I would like to be a scientist and learn lots of things.
When I grow up I would like to be a nurse and save lots of people's
lives.
When I grow up I would like to be a teacher and learn lots of things.
When I grow up I would like to be rich and get lots of things.

Lisa Marie Parkin (8)

What I Would Like To Be

When I grow up
I'd like to be a spy kid with climbing gadgets
Which act like magnets.

And a wheel looking switch
Which turns girls into a witch.

And the boss has an ant
Which acts like a robot wearing pants.

But if I get retired,
I'll get my dog,
And turn him to a hog.

Patrick Webster (8)

What I Would Like To Be

When I grow up I'd like to be a footballer
So I can take free kicks like David Beckham.
So I can go up front and I'd live in Peckham.
When I score a goal people will cheer.
After a goal I would drink beer.
At home I would step on my cat after it had caught a rat.

Mathew Iveson-Tong (8)

I Don't Know

What shall I do?
What shall I be?
Maybe a pop star, sing some songs.
Maybe an actor, acting my plays.
Maybe a teacher teaching best class of all.
Maybe a hero fighting the evil.
Maybe a vet saving animals' lives,
Or maybe a nurse helping the sick.
Or maybe a mother with just a few kids.
But whatever I would be and whatever I do,
I'll still be loved by my family.

Sophie Roberts (10)

Being A Gymnast

When I grow older I would like to be a gymnast,
I would do backward flips extremely fast,
I would do easy things and some really hard,
I would be able to do anything in my new leotard.
I would do different balances including an arabesque,
Cartwheels, flicks and things that I do best.
When I grow older I would like to fulfil my dream,
Becoming a gymnast and jumping off a beam!

Stephanie Homer (10)

I Want To Be . . .

I want to be a doctor
and always lend a hand.
I want to be a mermaid
and sit upon the sand.
I want to be a vet
and play with dogs all day.
I want to be a giant
and scare monsters away.
I want to be a teacher,
and teach subtract and add.
I want to be a witch
and be very, very bad.
I want to be a fairy
and wave my magic wand.
And if I can't be that,
I want to be James Bond.
There are so many things I want to be,
For now I think just be me.

Freya Lowden (9)

Super Heroes!

One day I had a dream
Had a dream
Had a dream
One day I had a dream
It was so very super.

The dream I had was so cool
So cool
So cool
The dream I had was so cool
It was all about some heroes.

I was a hero as well
As well
As well
I was a hero as well
And fighting crime I was.

There was a giant bug thingy
Bug thingy
Bug thingy
There was a giant bug thingy
Which I tore right in half.

Because I had saved the day
Saved the day
Saved the day
Because I saved the day
I got a golden medal.

When the day was over
Was over
Was over
When the day was over
I suddenly woke up.

Will I get another dream
Another dream
Another dream

Will I get another dream
And will it be as good?

Alexana Blott (10)

Hullabaloo Island

In the land of Hullabaloo
The people read, write and glue.
They wear yellow, white and blue,
They never will be late for the day
They ride a canoe.
They sleep with warm kangaroos
But never be late for a poetry train.
In the island of Hullabaloo.

Katy Jones (8)

In The Future

In the future I'm going to be a scientist
No thanks, it's not me.

A superstar
No I can't keep up with all the fast cars.

A policeman
No I might get run over by a van.

A weather girl
No it would be boring telling people
About weather in the world.

In the future I'm going to be
An actress, yeah, that's me.

Aimee Bambury (10)

I Want To Be A Witch

I wish, I wish I was a witch
And I had a magic wand.

I'd turn my brother into a frog
And my dad into James Bond.

If I had a broomstick
I'd fly to school each day.

From high up in the sky
I see my teacher on the way.

Katy Wallace (7)

Poems

One day I was playing for West Ham,
I was very happy
But where's my friend Sam?
Then I saw a bird, and its wings were very flappy.

I went down to my shed,
Then I saw a man,
He was very weird, because he had no head
Then he came out of the shed and drove a van.

Bradley Palmer (9)

My Future

I want to be famous
That's a fact.
To sing and dance,
And maybe act.
To go to London
In a show
Then to Hollywood
You never know.
And when I'm famous,
You will see
How proud my mum and dad will be.

Lucy Hines (7)

Tomorrow's World

If I were a scientist
My spacecraft would be the giantest,
And when I went to Mars
I saw lots of stars.
I discovered the sun
But it wasn't very fun.
In tomorrow's world I saw a phone,
That turned into a pine cone.

James Lawless (8)

I Want To Be A Vet

When I'm older I want to be a vet,
And have a dog called Bet.
A cat called Fluffy,
And even a crocodile with sharp teeth called Buffy.

Parrots that sing,
Monkeys that are proud and say Kerching.
Hyenas that laugh,
And zebras that get in the bath.
Giraffes with long necks,
And two fish called Posh and Becks.

Emily Fyffe (8)

Swimming With Dolphins

I have a dream to do one day
To go far away and play.
To swim with the dolphins in the sea
To have great fun, just them and me.
The water swishing, just me wishing.
I hope I have a dolphin of my own.
Their little tails go swish, swash, swosh.
A little shark comes to scare us off.
I fly through the water on my dolphin's fin.
This is a race now, and we're going to win!
We're safe now. We won the race,
My dolphin has a special smile on his face.
We had a cuddle, he felt shiny, soft and wet!
I wish this beautiful creature could be my pet!
That moment went so slow,
I knew it would soon be time to go.
I wish I had a dolphin of my own,
I promise I'll come back soon.

Hannah Davies (7)

I Dream Of Becoming Rich

I dream of becoming rich
I dream about it every day
If I was rich I would
Sing and play all day.

And I would go to the moon
With my rich chair
And come back home
And comb my hair.

I would like to go to the zoo
And ride on a bear
And go back to my palace
And I won't care.

And I will buy my favourite dog
It is so very fluffy
And I will name it Muffy.

Toni Campbell (9)

My Ambition

My greatest ambition is to keep horses
I'd take them to shows and ride them round courses.
I'll feed them, groom them, muck out too,
And take them to blacksmiths to get new shoes.
I'll clean their tack until it's shining bright
They will play in the fields from morning to night.
Hard work's involved but how great it would be,
If my ambition happened to me.

Emma Mitchell (9)

I Want To Be A Buiilder

Hammers clanking,
Hacksaws sawing,
Building a new bank,
That old crane clanks.

Buildings are made,
Each a new shade,
There are a few cranes,
Building new lanes.

Robert Kerry (9)

Springtime In The Future

Trees shaped as ice cream cones
Leaves shaped as mobile phones
Flowers that never die
Never-ending apple pie.
People whizzing as fast as cheetahs
Cuddly rabbits as personal heaters
The grass is pink
A world is made of rainbow ink.

Amanda Mowforth (8)

When I Am Twenty-Eight

When I am twenty-eight
I'll be as good as David Beckham at football.
I'll score a billion goals a season.
I'd get six billion pounds an hour.
I'll wish the Gauls, the Romans and Celts were alive.

George Taylor (7)

Year 3000

Floating houses
Floating cars
Witches on brooms
Riding to their tombs
The moon made of cheese
Holidays in space
Flowers that never die
Aliens come from space
And zombies and ghouls
The moon is a planet to live on
The sun is jelly
Pluto is warm
But that's all I can tell you
So I'll see you again in the year 3000.

Chantal Taylor (8)

When I Grow Up

When I grow up
I wish to be a football star
And play for the best team
I wish to be with the best players
And win all the cups
To win the league
Then we will win
And be called champions.

Kamal Samsudeen (8)

I Wish I Was A Horse Rider

I wish I was a horse rider
Going over all those jumps
They would be amazingly high
Just enough to touch the sky.
I would call my horse Hazel Nut.
I would go in competitions and win each
And every race.
We could ride through the fields
Under the moon
Pass the Butterfly house
All the way home again!

Bethany Parry (8)

Hover Board

One day I wished for a hover board and a wand
I stopped wishing before I went crazy.
The next day it came true
My wand was lying below my bed.
Outside my window was my board.
I hope it can do magic
And take me anywhere.

Finlay Douglas (7)

When I Grow Up

When I grow up I wish to see,
The moon with intelligent life.
When I grow up I wish to see,
No more guns blasting.
When I grow up I wish to see
Hover boards speeding down the track.
When I grow up I wish to see,
Cars, with no wheels.
Blasting off at rocket speed.

Christian Sloan (8)

Witch's Unknown Well

What is down the witching well?
Maybe a witch's unknown spell.
Spiderwebs and bath bubbles
Crackling like stew.

What is down the witching well?
Maybe a witch's unknown spell,
Big lumps of purple slime
Just waiting to explode.

What is down the witching well?
Maybe a witch's unknown spell.
A lava pit with hot sauce can only be put out by water.

What is down the witching well?
Maybe a witch's unknown spell.

Ross Churn (8)

A Dream Of The World

I wish the rain was food.
I wish that I could fly.
I would like to touch the sky
And see my family like flies.
I wish that animals could fly
And that no one would die.

Natasha Carr (6)

I Had A Dream

I had a dream I was working with turtles.
I had a dream I was swimming with dolphins.

I had a dream I found a mosaic,
from many layers of earth and soil.

I had a dream that I was flying in a hot air balloon,
flying with the birds.

I had a dream I was looking after tigers.

I had a dream that I rescued a panda.

All these dreams that I have dreamt can be accomplished
if I try and try again!

Maddie Haggar (10)

Swimming With The Dolphins

When I grow up I would like to be
Swimming with the dolphins in the sea,

Oh such silky and smooth skin
Wouldn't I be lucky just to win,

A prize for one day
Without having to pay,

I would feel so free
Swimming in the sea,

With the dolphins!

Emma Turner (9)

My Dream

I would love to go to Australia,
Scuba-dive by the coral reef,
See all the tropical fish,
Clownfish and angelfish too.
Walking across the sandy beaches,
Soft on my feet,
Picking up pretty shells,
Seeing all the animals.
Kangaroos, dingos and lots more,
Holding koalas, so sweet,
Looking at all the sights,
Sydney Opera House, one of them,
How I would love to go there!

Lauren Taylor (10)

Untitled

When my team have a throw in,
I run down the line,
And I go to my mates,
'The ball is mine.'

When I have a shot,
And the ball goes in the net.
I bet, bet, bet, bet,
We win in the wet.

When we have a corner,
And the ball goes up in the air,
And I jump up
And it hits my hair.

James Kirkland

Man City Dream

M anchester City are in the Premiership,
A li Benarbia is a midfielder for Manchester City,
N ick Weaver is a good sub-goalkeeper,
C hristian Negouai comes from France and plays for Manchester City.
H aifa is a football team in Israel,
E yal Berkovic has scored six goals for Manchester City,
S ylvain Distin is a defender for Manchester City,
T ottenham Hotspur is a football team in the Premiership,
E verton are a football team Richard Dunne used to play for,
R ichard Dunne is a defender,

C harlton Athletic is another Premiership football team,
I reland is where Richard Dunne comes from,
T o play with these would be great!
Y es, that would be my dream!

Luke Harris (8)

Ballet Star

The curtains rise up
And guess who you see
Who's that dancing?
Oh look it's me
I point my toes and turn around
I curtsy low right to the ground
The music starts
They look at me
I like to dance
I feel so free
My friends are there
How proud they are
That I am now a ballet star.

Lydia Hearn (9)

I Wish I Was A Vet

I wish I was a vet
So I could be with the animals all day
The hop, hop of the rabbit
The slow, slow of the tortoise
And the horses, they go neigh, neigh!

I wish I was a vet
To be with the animals all week
With a giraffe so tall
And a mouse so small
And the guinea pigs go squeak, squeak!

I wish I was a vet
To be with the animals all year
To keep them well
And make them better
Wow! What a great career!

Amy Guinness (7)

The Dream For Me

The dream for me it would be
To fly around all day,
Sing in the sun,
Dance by the moon,
And then my mum would say
'Calm down girl and get to bed
Where you can have your dreams instead.'

Hannah Morgan (10)

Untitled

At a late teenager play keeper
For an English football team,
That's what I have to accomplish
Because that is my dream.
Goodwin, Goodwin, Goodwin,
That's what I'd like the fans to shout.
When I save a penalty the ball rushes
Through my fingertips and goes out.

At the late twenties, I would have then
Definitely reached my best
Like the keeper Buffon better than all the rest.
Achieving trophies for my amazing and outstanding saves,
Hearing the fans give lots of cheers, support and raves.

I retired from football just over ten years from now.
As I look back in the past, the first word coming to my
Head is wow!
I now manage the mighty and unstoppable Arsenal team
Yes ever one of the mean footballing machines.

Jordan Goodwin (10)

I Had A Dream

I had a dream one winter's night,
That cars could fly through stars,
The moon was full and very bright,
They travelled onto Mars.

They landed on the jewelled ground,
The people wore white suits,
Their houses glass and perfectly round,
And pipers playing flutes.

Was this a dream or was it real?
Can this be future life?

Kayley Ashdown (10)

I Want To Be An Actress

I want to be an actress
Ha, ha, hey
I want to be an actress
And act all day
I want to be an actress
'Cause it'll be fun
I want to be an actress
Tum te tum
I want to be an actress
And I still do so listen up, hey I mean you.

Stephanie Cawthorne (10)

I Wish To Be A Spacegirl

I wish to be a spacegirl
Floating, floating.

Or I could be a postgirl
Posting, posting.

Maybe I'll be a famous chef
Roasting, roasting.

Perhaps I'll be a dancer
Dancing, dancing.

I might end up a surgeon
Stitching, stitching.

But I am just a schoolgirl,
Wondering, wondering.

Jessica Marriott (10)

My Dream

My dream is to play cricket
And one day bowl on the Oval wicket.
I'd hit a six and then a four
I'd add a hundred to the score
And I could not ask for any more.

I bowled a ball it went wide,
So I changed my stride.
I bowled a full toss
The batsman was very cross.
Out!

Alex Jones (9)

When I Grow Older

When I grow older
And it's time to leave school
I would like to be able to travel the world.
I'd see lots of different countries and learn about them too,
Including lots of people, and how different they live from you.
I would like to go on safari or maybe join the army,
But whatever I decide I know I will never hide,
From a world that is so big and is just waiting for us to live.

Chloe Louise Parkinson (7)

I Want To Be A Hairdresser

I want to be a hairdresser, snip, snap, snop,
I want to be a hairdresser, snap, snop, snip.
I want to be a hairdresser, cut and blow dry,
I want to be a hairdresser tint and die,
I want to be a hairdresser and own my own shop
I want to do a perm and set and how about a crop
I'd like to do afro hair braid, plait and knot.
   I want to be just like my mum,
   I want to do the lot!

Hollie Savill (9)

In Space

I'd like to go into space one day
And explore a planet.

But can a rocket take me up there,
Can it,
Can it?

The glistening of the stars and moon,
How cool would it be?

One of my highest dreams is just to see.

Elisa Danks (9)

Bravery

One day I went to the fair
And you will never guess what was there.
An enormous roller coaster in the shape of a monster.
I said to my dad,
'It looks really bad,'
But I still went on anyway,
Because I didn't want to spoil the day,
Even though it was scary,
And I was a bit wary,
I was there,
   At the fair.

Shelby Danks (7)

My Family

The people I love,
Live far and near.
The people I love,
All share a tear.

Even though sometimes,
We don't get along.
We always make up
And the fighting has gone.

The people I love,
Live all over the universe,
There's my mum, dad and brothers,
Also the others.
There's my uncle and grandad too.

Even though my uncle and grandad
Don't live close to me in reality.
I do know where they're living,
They're living in me!

Aimee Cole (11)

I Want!

Want to own chocolate factories
    Want to be a surfing champ
        Want to own dolphins
            Want to own a zoo!
                Want to have thirty-seven ponies
            Don't want to pay for them!
        Want to marry Patrick Swayze
    Want a pet snake
Want my own back on the teachers

But I want never gets!

Jessica Cleghorn (8)

My Dream

I had a dream last night . . .
I was lying in the grotto,
A fairy gave me 'just one wish'
Next thing I had won the Lotto.
I saw myself standing on the stage being presented with my cheque
I thought of all the wonderful things I'd buy
What will I do next?
'Should I buy this? Or should I buy that?'
I boasted to my friends
'I'll buy whatever you wish,
Your wish is my command.'
I reached out to touch my cheque,
It disappeared before my eyes.
Then someone beside me spoke and to my surprise I woke.

Laura McGorty (10)

A Wish

If I had three wishes they would be to float in the stars
and be happy as could be.
I would look at their colour and see their mighty size,
I would float up above and look at the starry skies.

My second wish would be to swim under the deepest sea,
Discover things that haven't been found yet, which would be
very hard to get.
I would look at their world and see what it is like,
And make friends with the pike.

Since now my wishes are coming to an end
I'd make the last one good, as I will keep it as a friend,
So my wish will have to be having good health for many years,
And enjoy myself and be happy and cheerful.

Loirin Leonard (10)

If I Had Super Powers

If I had super powers,
I would fly to Mars,
And eat lots of chocolate bars,
And if anyone tried to stop me,
I'd zap them with my laser eyes!
Or throw custard pies.

I would save the world,
Fly round and round,
Moving swiftly without a sound,
I'd destroy the bad, and keep the good,
Wear a mask, cloak and hood.

I'd get rid of the things that make me mad,
No more sick and no more sad.
I'd take from the rich and give to the poor,
And never allow any more war.

Rosalind Todman (9)

A Football Player

When I was at school
I wanted to play pool,
My dad changed my mind,
Then I came to find
That I was better at *football!*

I wanted to play for a real club,
My mum said, 'You should play pool.'
So I joined a football club,
Whilst my dad went to the *pub!*

I carried on my dream,
The dream was now a theme.
I scored an own goal,
I kicked the wooden pole.
I want to play for Spurs,
I was a curse, I was bad luck,
My foot got stuck,
But I carried on my dream.

I wish!

James Chittock (10)

Top Of The Class

Liam is his name, being good is his game.
Edward Francis Junior School is where he excels,
Never a chance of being expelled!
Head of class, 3M is Mrs Moore,
Never afraid to give me a top score!
Never a dull moment,
But never any tears,
The children all listen with eager ears.

Liam Tibble (7)

Lots Of Sport

I want to be a super hero, super hero, super hero,
I want to be a super hero with super strength and might.

I want to play for Man Utd, Man Utd, Man Utd
I want to play for Man Utd,
because they are the best team.

Andrew Kerry (7)

A World Of Fame

Wouldn't it be great,
To enter the world of fame?
To have all the posters, books and shops,
Covered with your name.

Your own merchandise, like Harry Potter toys,
All over the world being sold.
And on them would be the best thing of all,
Your name embossed in gold.

I'd like to be the next big thing,
Or be the world's best public speaker.
Or perhaps someone from ancient times, like Archimedes,
And shout that famous word: 'Eureka'!

How fantastic it would be to discover something,
That no one has seen before.
But there might be a downside to being famous,
Like all the journalists turning up at your front door.

Yes, you have to admit that being famous,
Might bring your daily life to an end.
Being followed around by the news all the time,
And overhearing gossip that drives you round the bend.

But I think it would be wonderful,
To be the next Shakespeare or Keats.
Have loads of people wanting your latest book,
And queuing up in fleets.

Would you think of fame as pure paradise?
Or a nuisance, like a lingering, bad smell?
I wonder if I'll ever be famous,
Only time will tell.

Mrinalini Dey (12)

Mad Rush!

Builders start dead on eight,
Chaos at the Harman house,
New kitchen being built,
Sleeping quietly as a mouse
Mad rush!
Mad rush!

Cups of tea going out
Finish work at four o'clock
'Goodbye' says an Irish voice,
Coming from the garden.

'Finished for the day, without a doubt.'
I say
Mad rush!
Mad rush!

Calming down, peace at last,
Plop into a chair.
No more digging,
No more drilling,
No more tearing out of hair!

Mad rush!
Building work!

Fleur Harman (10)

Artist Sonnet

I am an artist
I have tone
I have a brilliant wrist
I have a mobile phone
I have a brush
I don't rush
I read and write
I have foresight
I'm curious of the world
I'm furious of my world
I have paints
I have no faints
I have tone
I am an artist.

Ineel Kler (10)

My Ambition

I want to be a singer like the ones on MTV
Be the centre of attention where all eyes are on me.
I want to be a singer and be up there with the stars
And then with all the money I would blow it on
fast cars.
I want to be a singer with fame and celebrities
And everyone would know me from Jay-Z to the honeybees.
I want to be a singer and I want to have it all
My life would be so cool I'd really have a ball.
So now I've told you my ambition
Please let me win this competition.

Ashleigh Adabra (11)

My Super Powers

I will fly through the air
Fly! Fly!
Look for evil to fight
Fight! Fight!
Protect the world from danger
Protect! Protect!
And use my incredible powers
Powers! Powers!

Rebecca Cook (10)

When I'm A Millionaire

When I'm a millionaire, I'll make myself Queen,
I'll live in a chocolate palace, the biggest you've ever seen.

When I'm a millionaire, in all schools kids will teach teachers
About things like dancing and football,
But not science or maths, they're uncool.

When I'm a millionaire I'll build a McDonald's for my friends and me,
Where all the food will be for free.

When I'm a millionaire, I'll travel round the world in my private jet,
And I'll have a flying unicorn as a pet!

It's a shame money doesn't grow on trees.

Rebecca Fairbank (10)

Sundown Song

As a lake and stream glitters in the sunlight.
Animals may be found.
Like horses and butterflies, hedgehogs too and lambs upon the downs.
As the wild sky with the frisky night coming on.
The clouds start to turn grey.
The owls begin to play.
It's tonight for today.

Leah Plumley (8)

I Would Like To Be A Millionaire

I would like to be a millionaire
And travel round the world.
I would travel to far places
That have never been found.
I would like to go to India, Africa and Spain
I would like to go to Hungary, Slovakia and Ukraine.

I would like to be a millionaire
And travel round the world
I would travel to far places
That has never been found.
I would like to go to the USA, Bolivia and France
But most of all I would like to meet
Some very famous stars.

Bethany Lindo (10)

A Real Magician

My name is Wizard Wimplop
I am one hundred years old
I can do spells upon spells
More than you can behold.

My spells are amazing
'Fantastic!' I am told.
I keep them all in a suitcase
A portable one which can fold.

I am a silly fellow
As silly as can be
When I've worked out another spell
I do a dance with glee.

Once I made an invention
An electronic cup of tea
When anybody says 'Wizard Wimplop!'
I'm there, for that's me!

Once I was playing with a potion
And set my lab on fire
And because of the wonderful emotion
The flames grew higher and higher

I was born to be famous
I was born for the world to know
I was born to make people laugh
Even if they're feeling low.

My name is Wizard Wimplop
I am one hundred years old
And now the poem's come to an end
I'm going to make it solid gold.

Sidi Bai (10)

Ambitions

My ambition's to be an author
And a farmer too.
That is what I want to do.

I'd think and work
Write all day
That is where I would stay.

I would care for my animals
Give them crops to devour,
Check them every hour.

My ambitions,
That's them.

Danielle Aucott (9)

Untitled

I'd like to be a pop star and sing with a puppy.
I'd like to do gymnastics or ride a bike.
I'd like to have a baby and this is when I'm a lady

Lucy Devlin (7)

What I Would Be When I'm Older

I would like to be a football player like Michael Owen,
Score some goals, many goals
Like a professional.

I would like to be an engineer like my dad,
Travel the places that he has been to
I would be very glad.

I would like to be an electrician
Fix some wires
I would have a screwdriver
And some pliers.

Kieran Hughes (10)

My Dream And Ambitions

Dreaming is what I do best
As sometimes they come true.
Dreaming never lets you down
So all you think of is true.
I dream about everything I want to do
What I think will be fun.
That way I will be never disappointed
If my dream does not come true.
I dream about going around the world
Making friends in every country.
I know this dream will never come true.
But, hey that's what dreams are for - dreaming.
My dreams and ambitions are just the same.
I would like to see the world peaceful.
That's an ambition of mine.
Another ambition is to do well at everything
And look after all my family.
Some people may say that's not an ambition,
But it's what I'd like to do.
I want people to be around for me
To see the good in me.
I dream to make a better world,
Maybe my ambition will come true.

Martin Venables (10)

Dreams And Ambitions

My dreams and ambitions are both the same,
Playing football in the perfect game.
I'd have only the best,
To beat all the rest,
Scoring goals is my dream.

If that all failed,
A sports coach I'd be.
If you don't believe me,
Just wait and see!
Training players is my dream.

You never know,
It might be,
That it all turns out,
To be a different life for me!

Jack Flavell (10)

I Have A Dream

I have a dream,
One simple dream.
As brilliant as double cream.
To win an Oscar, appear on TV
Or maybe even be the Queen.
To zap the people who think I am crazy
To stay alive like a fresh new daisy.
For my name to appear in an autograph book,
Oh how lovely I will look.
To be as rich as chocolate cake,
Terrific songs I shall make.
But now I am here just nearly ten,
So I am going to have to wait till then!

India Jarvis (9)

Excuses, Excuses!

Please Miss I forgot my homework
Please Miss I did too
Please Miss my dog ate mine
I dropped mine in the loo!
Please Miss mine got burnt
Please Miss I did mine!

Harriet Webster (11)

The World At Our Feet

It's twenty years ahead
And I jumped out of bed.

A novel I had written
Was out free with pairs of mittens.

I got £2.50
From every copy of 'Roman City'.

They rang me up some hours later,
My fingers trembling like water.

'Lad, you've got the very thing,
I think you're the next JK Rowling!'

If I could be a famous writer,
It would make my world much brighter!

James Golding (9)

My Dream

The golden stars impeccably floating above all knowledge,
The stadia that has had its own impression,
Would it be quite impossible?
To fulfil a dream of such impassive teamwork,
Passion rears your mind to such extents!
The fans clear the names of not you but those who walk alongside you,
The ball is passed to your feet,
The daylight shall spur you on,
The ball released,
Passion seeps,
Hear the rustling of the net!
Goal!
The dream of many has been fulfilled by one!
Me!

Isaac Lister (9)

Peace

We all need peace in the world
So it's time we get it now!
No more fighting and bombing
No more hunger, but how?

I get scared when I hear these things,
If only people can see,
If we combine our strength,
We could stop it, you and me!

Who cares about fame and fortune
At least we will do something good.
Let the world share, love and care
Because we should!

Jenine Carron (10)

The World At My Feet

If only I had the world at my feet,
I'd prance up the catwalk,
Famous people I would meet.

If only the world belonged to me,
I'd be playing for Arsenal,
At Highbury.

If only I could make a fresh start,
The world would love me,
I'd gain Brad Pitt's heart.

If only the world gave me a try,
I'd stop world hunger,
And no one would die.

Brooke Maddison (10)

Aliens

How do we know if there are aliens or not?
How do we know if there are none or a lot?

Aliens are creatures that cannot be seen,
Aliens can be friendly, aliens can be mean.

Aliens come from out of space
They might destroy the human race.

Aliens can have very funny-looking feet
How do we know what they eat?

Aliens, some believe live on Mars which is very hot
Shall I believe in aliens or not?

Husnain Nasim (10)

Living On A Desert Island

D esert islands are hot,
E ven in the sea,
S un shining all day long,
E normous heats all day,
R oaring out loud,
T ides coming up high.

I feel rather hot on a desert island,
S wimming in the sea,
L ovely and warm,
A nd on a desert island I feel rather hot,
N ever cold always hot
D esert islands are hot.

Gemma Grayston (9)

Untitled

My dream, my dream is becoming rich.
With a limousine for a car,
A palace for a house,
It would be cool to become rich.
With the money we could do
Spend it on a holiday in the Seychelles
Buy myself a new house by the sea
Oh! It sounds cool to become rich!

Shaunna Litterick (9)

Playing For Man United

Have you ever wondered about playing for Man Utd.
Passing the ball to Nicky Butt
Or scoring a goal in a minute.

The crowd cheering you on by shouting your name.
Then they stop as you hit the post.
You put your hand over your head as you walk in shame.

You wait for the goalie to kick the ball.
You then wait for the ball to come,
Then you kick it.
Goal! You can't believe you scored.

Shanice Ennis-Melhado (9)

The World At My Feet

With the world at my feet
I can do anything I like
I could make a difference
In my life.

I could change the world
Or release a book
I could be a scientist
Or have model looks.

I could be a hero
Fighting evil every day
I could be rich with a limo
And have servants to do what I say.

I could be an astronaut
And fly to the stars
I could be an actress
Or drive in a racing car.

I could be prime minister
I could be a pop star
I could win the Whitbread award
I could win an Oscar.

Those would all be great
But I want to do things a different way
I want people to know I've tried
That's all I need to say.

I have decided
I will have a go
I will do my best
To make a difference tomorrow.

Francesca McLoughlin (10)

If I Was Rich . . .

If I was rich then I'd buy a lovely new mansion
With roasting fires and gleaming windows.

If I was rich then I'd buy an immaculate red Ferrari
It would have 520 horsepower and 5474 engine capacity.

If I was rich then I'd buy a few exquisite players for Arsenal.
Like the astonishing Ronaldo and the bendy Beckham.

But if I was rich
I really would buy . . .

James Moore (10)

My Dream Adventure

I have a very queer dream,
I wish to sail in the bloodstream.

Down the nose and up the brain
A journey on the memory lane.

Sharing the eye's secret mission
Following the trail of vision.

Surfing on the waves of sound,
To go swirling round and round.

Via the neck, and in the chest
Into the heart, for a rest.

To the lungs for some air
Blowing bubbles everywhere.

On the stomach's slimy ride
Down the intestine I'd glide.

And when enough I've explored,
I may then, be getting bored.

So a climb, back to the head,
And into my cosy bed.

Alysha Bhatti (9)

My Dream

I want to be a cat
Sleeping on a soft mat
Here comes my owner
I'm getting a fuss.

I want to be a cat
Have sharp claws
Don't have to do anything
Not even go to school.

I want to be a cat
Don't have to wash
Be free
Don't even have to make my own tea.

I want to be a cat
My name is Kitty
But I know it is only just a dream
It is such a pity.

Kirsty Knowles (11)

Pop Idol

There I was walking into the room
Happy and nervous at the same time,
I had to sing,
I was going to sing my favourite song 'Ka-Ching'.
And oh I wanted to scream *'Ka-Ching'* afterwards.
I moved up to the last fifty, it was amazing
I couldn't believe it,
We had a great time celebrating,
With champagne and loads of people came.
We even invited Simon Cowell,
He couldn't come, who cares?
We had loads of fun anyway!

Isabella Sidenius (9)

Becoming Rich

The atmosphere was hot and tense.
It was not a matter of a few pence.
Sitting there I was anxiously
Waiting for the moment eagerly.

Then came the news like a flash,
I was the winner of a bundle of cash.
So thrilled then I was,
A great day indeed it was.

Thoughts crept into my mind,
They were all of different kind.
Seeing the world, living in a mansion,
Travelling in a limousine, going for parties.

I thought again of the less fortunate,
Helpless, homeless and in pain they were.
Could I help? I wondered to myself
And *yes* is the answer, said my inner self.

'At the end of the day,' I ask
'What is it to become rich?
Is it being kind and generous,
Which makes us rich by heart?'

Samyukta Aryasomayajula (10)

My Hopes And Dreams

The one thing in the world
I am determined to do,
Is save the lives of animals
Koala to kangaroo.

The one thing in the world
I am determined to achieve,
Is help starving children
Living in poverty.

The one thing in the world
Most important to me,
Is going round the world
Spreading happiness and peace.

Those things in the world
Can be changed so easily.
Why doesn't anyone bother,
Is the question that comes to me?

Sophie Cowen (10)

Dan The Racing King

Driving round the bend in my gold and silver car,
Now I'm on the last lap and I know I've not got far.
The car in front of me turns gently to the right,
He's going in the pit stop which is only just in sight.

A corner looms ahead and I know that I should brake,
Then I think of winning and choose to accelerate.
The corner was hard but I stayed upon the track,
I just whizzed past the pit stop; now there's no turning back.

A Ferrari ahead, a Subaru behind . . .
This requires driving the best of all mankind!
But still I near the finish within the first top three,
Now it's getting harder, just two other cars and me.

From third to second, and then on to first,
The pressure is so high I think I'm going to burst.
Everybody in the crowd, fat or thin, short or long,
All cry out with sheer delight the one and only chanting song:

'We all love the man in the gold and silver car,
He's the best in the world so come on, Dan-Hurrah!'

As I cross the finish line, can you guess where I came?
Just like my other races, it was exactly the same.
Well that's another victory I've slipped into the bag,
Yes, the race is over but there's no need to be sad.

As I step out from my racing car, my winner's trophy awaits.
Then the speaker announces who got second place.
When I stop the car, the press all crowding in,
I think of the headline 'Dan The Racing King'.

I can see the judge, he is only just in sight.
Out of his hand, springs a hopeful flash of light.
All the racers turn as he walks past,
But I know the trophy is mine because I was extra fast.

Daniel Corteville (10)

Ambitions

I have a few ambitions that I'd like to fulfil
I'd like to live in a castle, which stands on top of a hill.
I'd like to eat spaghetti, whilst standing on my head
I'd like to spread banana on slices of week-old bread.
I'd like to race for Britain, in three Olympic Games
I'd like to run around the zoo, calling the animals silly names.
I'd like to do the tango by standing on one leg.
I'd like to own a dozen cats and each one I'd call Meg!
I'd like to write a story one hundred pages long
I'd like to stand in my classroom, banging a great big gong!
I'd like to swim in treacle, how sticky it would be!
I'd like to be a monkey, swinging from tree to tree.
I'd like to sing an opera in the middle of the night
(I'd like to run from my neighbours when they're shouting out in fright!)
I'd like to play a football match along with Michael Owen
I'd like to own the most outrageous lime green mobile phowen!
I'd like to eat a pizza five hundred inches wide
(But if I did that on my own, I'd get a pain in my side!)

So most of all, the thing I'd like when the future comes around
Is for everyone to live together,
In peace
Safe and sound.

Robyn Brown (10)

My Dream Come True

One day my mum forced me to go to a singing contest
The name of it was Pop Idol Junior.
The funny thing was I won
And next thing I knew I was flying to
Australia.

They thought I was so good
I became a star!
I've been all around the world
I've probably been everywhere.

But the person I'd most like to thank is my mum
For without her where would I be?
Probably another dumb person
With the brain of a chimpanzee!

Ciara McGuinness (7)

Tiger

Jungle hunter
Wearing his stripy coat
Looking for his next meal.

His tail flickering on the ground
He sees the antelope
Slowly he moves towards his next meal.

Suddenly he pounces
Bringing the antelope down
Splitting the antelope's heart.

After his meal
The tiger relaxes
Stretching, yawning and falling asleep.

Anisah Butt (9)

Super Power

I want super
Powers

Why?
I want to fly
Across to Manchester
And be a hero
Why?
I want to
Be famous
And with
All my super
Powers I'd
Save the day
Why?
I want to
Be rich
And win
Every game I play
What?
Like millionaire.

Shazia Shabbir (7)

My Future

In my future
In twenty years time
I will live in a mansion
And my clothes will be worth over a dime.

My mansion will be brick-red
I will have two flights of stairs,
I will have six bedrooms,
And five toilets with posters of the Reds.

I will have a wonderful wife,
And two charming kids,
Who will be strong
And they will have an exciting life.

That is my future,
I hope it turns out right
And if it does,
My family will be a lovely sight.

Jasmair Purewal (10)

The Queen

I wish I were a queen
Who had magic powers
And ruled the world
In my giant towers.

Servants will serve me
With their delicious food
And if they don't
I will be very rude.

If I was the best
I would beat the rest
And if I was strong
I would do nothing wrong.

Fatima Jan (7)

As If I'm A Child In War?

Just for an hour,
I want to be a child in a war-torn country.
To make me appreciate all the things
I never count.
To make me thankful for my family when I get back home from school.
For the sisters I have whom I can argue and laugh with,
For all the food I usually don't want to eat,
Because I have choices,
And I can decide things for myself.
So I'm thankful that I am never alone.

Thank you Allah.

Mariam & Sara Jussab (9)

The Dream

I dreamed I was a teacher,
My name was Miss Beacher,
I had a class of thirty,
But I didn't teach them anything dirty.
I would never ever get the sack,
I was absolutely sure of that,
But I had to fight my temptation,
Of giving the children one big smack.
In the staffroom I had a drink or two,
Then I had to try not to go to the loo.
After this my dream came to an end,
So now I'm a normal child again.
Oh I nearly forgot to say it's bye from me,
Until we meet once again.

Harsimran Sandhu (11)

Rich As Rich

I wish I was rich
I wish I was rich
What if I was rich?
Rich as rich
One pail of gold
One pail of shiny gold
One pail of old gold.

Kaili Siwily (8)

The World

The world is fat, the world is short,
The world swirls you around like a dinosaur.
You should ignore it at all.
So you must not fall.

Amrit Athwal (7)

The World Goes Round

The world says *hello*, do we wake up?
No!
The world grows do we say no?
Everyone wonders upon the world, do you know?
How do we grow like fruits?
No
Just imagine being 40,075m long, do you care?
How about being 400 tonnes
Earth should be looked after like we are.

Harvandna Athwal (9)

My Dream Come True

I had a dream of being able to walk on to Pop Idol stage in ten years.
I hope to succeed and be the best I can be.
When I grow up I would like to be a pop star.
I would love to get lots of money and buy a Ferrari.
I would love to get a big house and get a karaoke in every room.
But now I'm ten and I will have to wait ten years for that dream to come true.

Emer O'Neill (10)

My Dreams

For hopes and dreams and lovely things and using our extremes.
I want to be a surgeon for completing my dreams.
Doing an operation is a real big thing, I might even cure a disease or something.
Being rich with fancy things with lots of dogs wearing earrings.
'How does it sound, Dr Wilson?
I think it sounds quite good.'
I might be successful, I might not.
I could be working in a shop.
And that is my dream to be a surgeon.
Nothing else for my future.

Adam Wilson (10)

My Dream

To be an electrician, that is my dream.
It is important to me, but to others it may not gleam.
While I'm fixing wires on the computer
Others might want to stand on Jupiter.
I want to fix games and PlayStations
So children can play their own imaginations.
I think it is exciting, to some it may not seem,
But to be an electrician that is my dream.

Eoin Farrelly (9)

My Dream

My dream is to be a pop star that walks up to the stage.
When I walk up to the stage
I see the people looking and I hear them screaming.
I am nervous at the start
But then the song pours out - from my heart.

Kerry Coyle (9)

Dream

Dreams of walking into the stadium of Old Trafford.
Playing with 68,079 fans looking at you.
Just thinking of it is great, marvellous, absolutely fabulous.
I would like to drive a Ferrari.
Live in a big house.
I might even get to play for Republic of Ireland.
Even play in a World Cup.
That would be my definite dream,
I sure hope it comes true.

Tom Caldwell (10)

Teaching Dreams

Dreams of being a teacher
Walking into class,
The children look at creatures
Salmon and seabass.
Science and English
History too.
A tin of scissors
Work hard you!

Rachel Stone (9)

My Future

I am on my way to adulthood
I am no longer a child
My future changed when I moved into university
This is what happens:

I won the lottery at the age of twenty-two.
I made donations to the poor.
I bought a kitten and named her Angel.
Fell off my garage roof and broke my leg, it was so sore.
I became a vet and helped many, many animals.
My Saturday job is at the RSPCA.

My future ends right here, I have no more to tell you.
Can you tell me about your future?

Tara Ingham (10)

My Future

I'm no longer in childhood
I play for Ipswich and England
I have four cars and a mansion in the sun
I won the lottery when I was twenty-three
And I gave it all to charities.

Joseph Brown (10)

I'm Climbing Hills To My Future

My journey of life has begun
I have travelled far and wide
Football is my life
As well as my beautiful wife.
My car is a Porsche Boxster
It shines with beauty.
My clothes are designer clothes,
My gold chains are pure gold,
And my mansion is made of marble.

Aaron Emeny (10)

Untitled

My future life will be like this:

When I am older I'll be buying a mansion
Also a brand new Porsche.
I'll be playing for England and Real Madrid.
I'll be a right winger
Then I'll buy a motorbike.
I'll be rich and famous
My name will be big in England and Real Madrid.

Reece Fortescue (10)

The World At Our Feet

I looked for a job in town.
There was an audition.
In the window of the New Look shop.
I went in and sang my favourite song.
I was only ten years old.
A letter arrived the next day.
I was through!
They gave me ten thousand pounds for my great performance.
The next day I went to the studio.
They have a song for me to sing.
I sing it.
At the end the studio people were in tears.
They'd loved it.
I'd become the most famous star in the world!

Emily Tricker (10)

My Narrow Path

My childhood has disappeared,
Now I can change my fate for the rest of my mysterious life.
There can be no future unless it finally opens up my feelings.
I can change and turn my life for the future awaits.
I won't give up.
In the darkness I must learn how to control my fate.
I have a secret life.
I right the wrongs with everyone knowing.
I must give the world a second chance.
My altered echo can turn the world on its feet.
I have made my choice, I need to keep it.

Jagger Creasey (10)

What Would You Wish For?

What would you like?
A football, a bracelet,
Or a really groovy bike.

What would you wish for?
What would be fun?
A ride on an elephant
Or a long day in the sun!

What would you wish for?
What would be best?
A trip into space and back,
Then finally a rest!

Lauren Brader (7)

Dolphins

Dolphins splash
Dolphins splish
Dolphins splash in the deep blue sea.

Dolphins splish
Dolphins splash
Dolphins come and swim with me.

Dolphins splash
Dolphins splish
You are as lovely as can be.

Jade Carter (7)

Fireworks

Fireworks, fireworks banging.
Fireworks, fireworks banging.
Sparkling in the sky.
They fly so high.
They're prettier than the morning sunrise.

Danáe McAvennie (7)

Oh, To Be An Actress

Oh, to be an actress
Would be a fantasy
To see all the crowds
Jumping up and down for me,
I'd be famous all around the world
From China to Brazil,
To be out on the town
With autograph books to fill.
I'd buy a limo, a sports car and a corvette,
I'd buy my mum and dad a house
And make sure it's the very best!

Dearbháile McKinney (10)

Powers

I wish I had powers
Which knocked down big towers
I wish I could fly
And fight with an evil guy.

Evil I would fight with my bare small hands
and fight on different beachy lands.
I'll save the world within the time
then I'll win a golden dime.

I'm beautiful and strong
but I'm not that long
my dream is important so is my beauty
but I'm always on time for my duty.

I'll wait for now in my house
with my small brand new mouse
near the window, I shall stare
but that's the thing I really can't bear.

Aisha Iqbal (11)

Actress

I will grow up to be
A crowd thriller
Who will be a smile bringer
To all households
I will be voted the sweetest presenter.

Stembeni Mahachi (9)

My Way Of The World

When I grow up, I'd like to be
A BMX rider
That the world could see
I'd jump up and down
And do many tricks
I'd fly through the air
And jump over bricks!

I'd like to compete against the best that there is
And go around like a bit of a whizz.
People would remember me as the best
And then I'd have a little rest.
I'd miss my family and all the rest
But they would be proud
If I was the best.

Jordan Differ (10)

My Dream . . .

I would like to be a singer or maybe a swimmer
Or win a trophy in a Grand Prix.
Go to college or university
That's what I want to do.

Then again maybe a fearless hunter
I'll find the abominable snowman or a pet detective
I'd find the Loch Ness monster too
These are other things I dream of doing.

Or I just might settle for doing my homework
And handing it in on time.

Jonathan Priestly (9)

Football Dream

I would like to play for a football team,
for that is my greatest dream.
I love to hear a crowd scream
when I score for my team.

I would like to play with many teams
but Manchester Utd is my dream.
The way they play encourages me,
to play like Ruud van Nistelrooy.

It is not for the money
playing football is my dream,
but it couldn't take me away
from my family and friends.
That is something nothing can take its place.
In the time I will be fine if I have to leave home.

Nimrit Dhillon (10)

Future Dreams

Hello, my name is Amy
I like to run around
I want to be a star and it's not far
The world at our feet
So listen to the beat
Design some clothes
And touch my toes
To grow flowers
I have powers
So listen to the beat
The world at my feet
Play and jump and get a bump
But I am, hooray!
Animals and pets, I like baguettes
Hooray! Hooray! Hooray!
The world at our feet
So listen to the beat
Go on holiday
Sitting in the sun,
Let's have fun,
The world at my feet
So listen to the beat,
Now I really need to stop
I'll see you later and watch the clock
The world at our feet.

Amy Mackenzie (9)

My Future

I'd love to be a lady advocate, actress and an author,
So many things to do,
I'd love to make the world war free and safe,
All for me and you.

I'd love to marry a movie star and drive in a flash car,
I'd love to have three children, Sarah, Louise and Paul.
I'd love them to grow up and be quite tall!

I'd love to build my own mansion overlooking the sea,
I'd love my own private pool and swim in it every day.
I'd love two cats and a Labrador,
A small white cat called Sugar and a ginger cat called Spice.
A female dog called Pluto with brown eyes!

I'd give some of my money to war shattered countries
I'd make a movie about them too!
I'd give them clothes, toys, pots and pans,
I'd give them bed linen too!

These are all the things I'd love to do,
They may or they may not come true,
It would be fun to win an Oscar or be a model,
I haven't a clue what to do!

Kirsty McDermott (10)

The Way Of The World

I would like to drive a Ferrari
Because I would share it with them, my family.
I would like to get stuck on a desert island with a spaceship,
I would like to share a flat with Jordan and Aaron.
I will be a tree climber.

Rory King (10)

My Future Dream

I want to be a nursery teacher
and just hope they do not bring in a creature,
I'll bring in a big bear
just so they think it's fair.

I would like to see a chocolate bar
and maybe even sing with a superstar.
I would like to see so far
and maybe even drive a car.

I would like to see a plane,
sometimes they steer in the rain.
In the aircraft some people die in pain,
and they make Cola out of a cane.

My heart is beating
as I think about this competition
Last night I got permission
as I enter the poet competition!

Lauren Clayden (10)

My Dream

What do you want to be when you grow up?
People ask you when you're small,
You stand there quite astonished,
Because you've no idea at all.

But now I'm a little older
And know what I'd like to be,
I want to dig and find things,
In lands across the sea.

I want to be an archaeologist,
You may ask me why,
I just love ancient history,
All about times that have gone by.

To find a hidden artefact,
For centuries undiscovered underground,
Would be the greatest thing for me,
I'd jump and run around.

I'd write books and give lectures,
To learned people across the land,
Of things I had discovered,
And held in my hand.

I will work hard at my lessons now,
And make my knowledge vast,
Then I can achieve my dream
And discover something of the past.

Carol-Ann McCorgray (9)

My Dreams

What should I be?
A lawyer or a writer,
A wrestler or a fighter,
Maybe win an Oscar,
Save a life or be a doctor,
Be a teacher,
Have a pet or a creature,
Play football,
With the team and all
Go to college or university?
If I could I would do all of these things today
But I can't, I just remembered
Maybe I'll just feed a leopard!

David Currie (9)

Untitled

My greatest dream is to stay friends with everyone in my class.
That would be the greatest thing ever.
But this class will be split up
But I can still be in contact.
But most will get their dreams
So I will lose my friends and I will be sad.
I will not waste the time I have with them
That is my greatest dream.
So I will treasure my moments with them.

Lewis Blaney (9)

My Dreams And Wishes

I'd dream to fly in a fighter plane
Flying higher than the tallest crane
Soaring, diving, whirling,
Looking down on Stirling.
I wish I had magic powers
Turning paper into flowers
Walking high in mid-air
Making people turn and stare!

Jamie Sivewright (9)

Dream Of The World

In the future there shall be
Superheroes and stuff and really cool things,
But what I think we would all like would be . . .
No poverty and all our dreams to come true,
With enough food and water for the whole world
To eat and drink so that they'll be good and strong.
My dream is to have a boat and a nice car.

Tom Westland (10)

I Wish, I Wish, I Wish

I wish I had a PlayStation 2,
I wish nobody was hungry,
I wish I didn't have to feed the dogs,
I wish I had a football field in the garden,
I wish I lived next to the sea and it was warm.
I want to be a games designer,
I want to be a blacksmith,
I want my friends nearby,
I want the sun to shine all summer,
And no school,
No homework,
Just fun, fun, fun.

Mungo Dewar (10)

Untitled

My ambition is to be a McDonald's maker,
My ambition is to be a wood maker,
My ambition is to be a film star,
My ambition is to be a pop star,
My ambition is to be a baker,
My ambition is to be a toy maker,
My ambition is to be a traveller,
My ambition is to be a messenger,
My ambition is to be an actor,
My ambition is to be a china doll,
My ambition is to be a frame maker.

Rhianne Spence (10)

I Want To Be A Vet

'Mum, Mum, I want to be a vet.'
'But don't you want to fly a jet?
Don't you want to be a nurse,
Or even drive a hearse?
You could be a teacher for Key Stage 2,
Or train the chimps at Chester Zoo.'
'Mum, Mum, I want to be a vet,
Because it is the best job yet.'
'You could join the police and be a cop,
Or sell sweets in a sweetie shop.
You could study drama and be an actor,
Or farm the land and drive a tractor.'
'We'll have to see which job I get,
But Mum, *I want to be a vet.'*

Natalie Bould (10)

RSPCA Inspector

R SPCA inspector is what I aim to be,
S nakes and spiders are not for me,
P eople are so cruel to pets,
C are and love from me they'll get,
A lost dog, an injured cat,

I can always handle that.
N ursing a newborn baby foal,
S aving a squirrel or even a mole.
P rotecting animals from all harm,
E ven when they bite your arm.
C aring for animals is what I do,
T o be the one dressed in blue.
O ff I drive in my van,
R SPCA, yes, I'm your man!

Liam Thomas (10)

My Hopes And Dreams

To be an engineer my ambition is . . .
To be the best one, an engineering whizz.
To follow in my dad's footsteps would make him proud,
He'll be cheering me on really, really loud.

One day, maybe I hope I will play
For the Shrewsbury Hockey team.
And then I'll ask someone to pinch me
So I know if it's a dream.
Everyone will be cheering for me saying,
'Come on Zach.'
Andy my coach will be jumping up and down
Saying, 'Give the ball a whack.'

In the future I dream of going to Japan
I'd like to go with my girlfriend
That's the plan.
That's all in my future for now I can just dream.
Because life is full of surprises and they're not always
What they seem.

Zach Said (10)

Author

B is for best, I'll be the best
O is for original, I'll write lots of books.
O is for over, my books will be read over.
K is for kingdom, books read everywhere.

Elizabeth Beesley (11)

Jobs

Jobs we go to work
And people get money.
Jobs are for money
To get a better job.
Jobs are for education
For all other people.
Jobs are for more than one person
To get the job done.
Jobs are for exercise
For you and others.
Jobs there are lots of them,
But which one will I have?
I'll think about that later.

Jordan McMicklewright (10)

The Man U Match

It's 3pm and the whistle blows,
It's a free kick to Man U.
The striker gets the ball and goes for a run,
Then West Brom get the ball and show them how it's done.

Our striker, Rob Hulse sprints to the net,
The crowd stand up and shout, 'Get it in!'
He shoots, he scores,
It's back to the start.

All the players make a plan,
Man U running forward to shoot a goal.
The whistle goes four times, it's 1-0 to West Brom,
They have won the FA Cup!

Rebecca German (10)

My Dream - The Roller Coaster Tester

Waiting to board this metal beast,
Slowly but surely I am pulled along.
Checking the bolts are all well greased
And safety belts are where they belong.

Excited and scared all in one go,
Round the loops and bends.
Up very high then drop low,
Testing out the latest trends.

But being a roller coaster tester
Can be cool but dangerous.
Even on the rushing 'Cresta',
The fear can be infectious.

Dark tunnels, wet log rides,
White water rafting.
Checking for leaks on the water plume sides,
This is all too daring!

Lucas Palmer (11)

Scuba Duba!

I want to see the ocean worlds,
The world under the waves.
I want to see a Pufferfish,
Have time to stop and gaze.

I want to see creatures of the deep,
All strange shapes, large and thin.
I want to see a jellyfish,
See how fast dolphins swim.

I want to swim the icy waters,
See tiny penguins grow.
I want to see a baby walrus,
Or seals down below.

I want to see the seagulls swoop,
Catch a fish or two.
I need to see an Albatross egg,
I'd like to hold it too.

The Red Sea in Egypt,
Has coral reefs galore.
I want to scuba-dive down there,
See the Saber Squirrel fish and more . . .

All these things I want to do,
All include the sea.
If I become a scuba-diver,
You'll rarely see me!

Hannah Skeggs (10)

Triceratops Dreams

My dream is to see the world,
And dig up a dinosaur.
Perhaps a triceratops or even an allosaurus,
Or maybe a utahraptor that leaps and kicks.
But I would like to find a archaeopteryx.

There's just one problem,
Where to begin.
Maybe the Gobi where the sand is thin.
Then again all they found there were eggs,
I'd much rather go to Utah and find some T-rex legs.

Oh help! Some dinosaur bones are massive!
How would I get them in a truck?
It looks like I've run out of luck.
And most fossils are in places I can't even say.
Oh well it was an exciting dream anyway.

Catherine Bralesford (11)

I Wish I Could Swim With Dolphins

I wish I could swim in the deep,
With these good-natured mammals.
Gliding through the frothy waves,
Upon a dolphin's back.

Clinging to their soft grey skin,
Jumping out of the water for joy.
Flapping their tails up and down,
Gracefully showing their fins.

Ballerinas of the ocean,
Dancing on crisp icy waves.
Diving down to fountains of coral,
Elegant, intelligent and brave.

Elizabeth Metcalfe (10)

Dreaming

I would like to be
A writer.
I would write an inspirational book,
Maybe meet someone famous
And write about their life.

If I did, I would like to meet
Jennifer Lopez, Gareth Gates,
Or maybe even Cat Deeley.

Also, I would like to be
A model
And live in a small cottage.
Each day I would walk down the catwalk,
Everyone clapping and cheering.

These are the things I dream each day,
That I would like to come true!

Rachel Muirhead (9)

In The Future

In the future
I want to see,
What has actually
Become of me.

Maybe I could be
A famous singer,
Or maybe I could be
A famous swimmer.

Maybe I could go up
In an air balloon,
Or maybe I could see
A real live baboon.

Maybe I could be
A well-trained teacher,
Or maybe I'll become
A wildlife creature.

Maybe I could climb a tree,
Or maybe I could stroke a bee.

Maybe I could be
A babysitter,
Or maybe I could be
A school shoe fitter.

In the future
I want to see,
What has actually
Become of me.

Jasmine Bradbury (9)

Future

In the future I'd like to be . . .
A sailor who sails to sea
A mountain climber, climbing high
A high jumper and touch the sky
In the future I'd like to be
A shopkeeper who sells ice cream
A footballer, scoring goals
A miner digging coal
In the future I'd like to be
A woodcutter cutting down trees
A rugby player scoring tries
A policeman detecting lies.

Amy Elder (10)